Ritual Textuality

O | R | S   Oxford Ritual Studies

Series Editors
Ronald Grimes
Ute Hüsken, University of Oslo
Eric Venbrux, Radboud University Nijmegen

THE PROBLEM OF RITUAL EFFICACY
Edited by William S. Sax, Johannes Quack, and Jan Weinhold

PERFORMING THE REFORMATION
Public Ritual in the City of Luther
Barry Stephenson

RITUAL, MEDIA, AND CONFLICT
Edited by Ronald L. Grimes, Ute Hüsken, Udo Simon, and Eric Venbrux

KNOWING BODY, MOVING MIND
Ritualizing and Learning at Two Buddhist Centers
Patricia Q. Campbell

SUBVERSIVE SPIRITUALITIES
How Rituals Enact the World
Frédérique Apffel-Marglin

NEGOTIATING RITES
Edited by Ute Hüsken and Frank Neubert

THE DANCING DEAD
Ritual and Religion among the Kapsiki/Higi of North Cameroon and Northeastern
Nigeria
Walter E.A. van Beek

LOOKING FOR MARY MAGDALENE
Alternative Pilgrimage and Ritual Creativity at Catholic Shrines in France
Anna Fedele

THE DYSFUNCTION OF RITUAL IN EARLY CONFUCIANISM
Michael David Kaulana Ing

A DIFFERENT MEDICINE
Postcolonial Healing in the Native American Church
Joseph D. Calabrese

NARRATIVES OF SORROW AND DIGNITY
Japanese Women, Pregnancy Loss, and Modern Rituals of Grieving
Bardwell L. Smith

MAKING THINGS BETTER
A Workbook on Ritual, Cultural Values, and Environmental Behavior
A. David Napier

RITUAL TEXTUALITY
Pattern and Motion in Performance
Matt Tomlinson

RITUAL TEXTUALITY

Pattern and Motion in Performance

MATT TOMLINSON

OXFORD
UNIVERSITY PRESS

OXFORD
UNIVERSITY PRESS

Oxford University Press is a department of the University of
Oxford. It furthers the University's objective of excellence in research,
scholarship, and education by publishing worldwide.

Oxford   New York
Auckland   Cape Town   Dar es Salaam   Hong Kong   Karachi
Kuala Lumpur   Madrid   Melbourne   Mexico City   Nairobi
New Delhi   Shanghai   Taipei   Toronto

With offices in
Argentina   Austria   Brazil   Chile   Czech Republic   France   Greece
Guatemala   Hungary   Italy   Japan   Poland   Portugal   Singapore
South Korea   Switzerland   Thailand   Turkey   Ukraine   Vietnam

Oxford is a registered trademark of Oxford University Press
in the UK and certain other countries.

Published in the United States of America by
Oxford University Press
198 Madison Avenue, New York, NY 10016

CIP data is on file at the Library of Congress

ISBN: 978–0–19–934113–9 (hbk)
ISBN: 978–0–19–934114–6 (pbk)

1 3 5 7 9 8 6 4 2
Printed in the United States of America
on acid-free paper

Contents

List of Figures

Preface

THIS BOOK IS based on twenty-eight months of research conducted in Fiji between 1996 and 2011. In Tavuki Bay, Kadavu Island, I carried out village-based ethnographic fieldwork during parts of 1996, 1998–1999, 2003, and 2005–2006. In Suva, Fiji's capital, I conducted ethnographic and archival research during parts of 2008, 2009, 2010, and 2011.

My primary fieldwork method is to record and analyze speech, primarily speech during church services. In doing so, I aim to understand people's beliefs and practices regarding religious authority and the efficacy of ritual. In archival research, too, I focus on the ways that language is used for religious purposes. My justification for taking this approach is that in Christianity in Fiji—and especially in Methodism, the focus of most of my work—a sense of effective religious practice depends heavily on the use of particular forms of speech. Eventful things like sermons, prayers, and storytelling are the vital substance of Fijian Methodism; they are what make religion matter to people. In Chapter 2, I tell the story of being dazed by my encounter with Pentecostalism at a riotous "crusade" in a public park, an event in which Christianity's sensational embodied elements came to the fore: running and dancing, raising hands to heaven, and applauding God loudly and often, a style of worship sharply different from that of Methodism. Even as I appreciated the force of such intensely embodied practices, however, I could not help but notice that the Pentecostal preacher's speech—specifically, his sermon and altar call—played the pivotal role in turning all of that kinetic energy into a coherent ritual event that was meant to be considered an effective encounter with divinity.

Each of the following chapters is based on a different kind of relationship with the communities involved. In Chapter 2, I was a detached observer at a public event. I stood and clapped along with the Pentecostals, but I am not Pentecostal myself, I did not speak in tongues, and I did not get dunked in the baptism tank. My approach to the performance, in which I focus strictly on the textual patterns unfolding in the preacher's speech, might frustrate readers who want a vivid account of the physically exuberant, passionate, and demanding practices through which one seeks salvation in Pentecostalism, but I cannot pretend to know that kind of experience; I simply hope that the account I offer of Brother Colegrove's preaching and altar call will interest those who realize there is hidden dynamism in the text on a page. In studying kava-drinking sessions, the subject of Chapter 3, I have always been an enthusiastic participant-observer. I have drunk kava in forty-five different villages and settlements in Kadavu, as well as in Suva, Australia, New Zealand, and the United States, observing differences and similarities in ritual practice. In drinking kava so often, I have come to marvel at the range of interaction styles possible around the bowl, from vigilant and reverential stillness to carefree joy. The examination of "happy deaths" in Chapter 4 is based primarily on research conducted at the National Archives of Fiji, the Mitchell Library in Sydney, and St. Mark's National Theological Centre Library in Canberra, with the final section of the chapter drawing on ethnographic fieldwork conducted in Kadavu in 2003. The analysis of monologue in Chapter 5 is based largely on mass-media accounts of events in Fiji since the coup of 2006. Thus my social location and analytical perspective shifts considerably over the course of the following chapters, although the way I handle data—the voices I quote, the events I focus on—is shaped by my overall experience of research in Fiji.

Because my method of analysis is text-based, many Fijian-language phrases and passages appear in the following pages. In the standard orthography for Fijian,

> *b* is pronounced /mb/ as in slu*mb*er
> *c* is pronounced /th/ as in *th*is
> *d* is pronounced /nd/ as in la*nd*ing
> *g* is pronounced /ng/ as in si*ng*er
> *q* is pronounced /ngg/ as in fi*ng*er

Most of the Fijian-language texts presented here are in the national standard version of the language, although some include features of the Kadavu dialect, for which I use *j* for /ch/ as in *ch*eek, reflecting local pronunciation. I do not use macrons to indicate long vowels, although when quoting sources that use macrons I retain them. In quoting English-language newspapers from Fiji, both print and online versions, I have usually edited minor typographical errors without adding [*sic*].

I have taken all of the photographs that appear in this book. They have been cropped, digitally color-corrected, and cleansed of dust and scratches, but not otherwise altered. The map of Fiji was prepared by the CartoGIS team at the Australian National University's College of Asia and the Pacific.

Acknowledgments

FUNDING FOR THE research on which this book is based came, in chronological order, from the Department of Anthropology at the University of Pennsylvania; an International Dissertation Research Fellowship from the Social Science Research Council; Bowdoin College; Monash University; and a Discovery Project grant from the Australian Research Council (#0878736). The generosity of all of these sources is gratefully acknowledged.

Versions of Chapter 2 were presented in seminars at the University of Melbourne in 2010 and Monash University in 2011, parts of Chapter 3 were presented at the conferences of the Pacific History Association in Suva in 2008 and the Australian Anthropological Society in Perth in 2011, and a version of Chapter 5 was presented at the Australian National University in 2012. I thank all of the audiences at these events for their thoughtful feedback. An earlier version of Chapter 4 was published in 2007 as "Publicity, Privacy, and 'Happy Deaths' in Fiji," *American Ethnologist* 34(4): 706–720, and the first epigraph to Chapter 5 is reproduced from *The Dialogic Imagination: Four Essays* by M. M. Bakhtin, edited by Michael Holquist, translated by Caryl Emerson and Michael Holquist, copyright 1981, and used by permission of the University of Texas Press.

Since I began research, the list of people in Fiji who have helped me has grown ever longer, and my appreciation for their generosity and patience has intensified with time. For nine months between 2008 and 2011, I was based at the Pacific Theological College in Suva and enjoyed its vibrant intellectual climate and warm loloma. At PTC, I owe a special debt of thanks to the principal, Fele Nokise, and his wife Roslyn, as well as Manfred Ernst, Tevita Havea, and Kafoa Solomone. I also owe a long-term debt to the church leaders, chiefs, and people of Tavuki Bay in Kadavu, including the paramount chief during my fieldwork in the 1990s and 2000s, the late Vunisa Levu, Tui Tavuki, Ratu I. W. Narokete. All have been kind beyond measure. I emphasize that no individuals at PTC or in Kadavu are responsible in any way for the views I express in this book, including my analysis of Fiji's political situation in Chapter 5.

For comments on the manuscript, I am grateful to Ilana Gershon, Julian Millie, Gerry Schramm, Kristina Wirtz, and Robert Wolfgramm, all of whom offered observations and suggestions that reshaped the final product. In addition, Michael Lempert and Chris Gregory offered advice at crucial stages of the project that helped me clarify the argument and see its possibilities as well as its limits more clearly. I have also benefited from the generosity of Andrew Arno, "Apo" Aporosa, and Guido Carlo Pigliasco, who have graciously shared their expertise and thereby helped sharpen the argument in these pages. Michelle O'Toole and Timothy Clarke at Monash University provided excellent research assistance, and Cynthia Read and her assistants Sasha Grossman and Marcela Maxfield at Oxford University Press were both expert and encouraging. I am also thankful to the series editors, Ronald L. Grimes and Ute Hüsken, for their support. My sincere thanks to all.

Finally, I must thank my wife Sharon and our sons, Andrew Cayo and Evan Leo, for their beautiful hearts and boundless energy across countries, years, and projects. This book is dedicated to them.

Ritual Textuality

I

Into Motion

IN ANTHROPOLOGY, MOTION is a dominant metaphor of the times. Humanity swims in "global flows," global interconnections generate "friction," and the classic concept of culture is newly "public, mobile, traveling." As a result, anthropologists need to position themselves in new ways to observe movement in social life. Some situate themselves as "dwellers" in ever-shifting borderlands, others as scientists in search of culture's "laws of motion."[1]

In calling attention to the creativity and instability of social life, one may find metaphors of motion useful, but they can also be misleading. "Metaphors are dangerous things that prove nothing," Edward Sapir wrote almost a century ago, although he hastened to add that the particular metaphor he was examining—culture as a plant growing in the rich soil of history—had "soundness" (1924: 418). Like all metaphors, metaphors of motion offer some new insights by limiting others. Their revelations are always partial, and if metaphors of motion are used in loose, unreflective ways, they run the particular risk of portraying sociocultural processes at a rarefied level that seems to be independent of individuals' actions (Rockefeller 2011).

In this book, I use the metaphor of motion, but in perhaps a counterintuitive way. I analyze ritual performances by focusing on the motion of signs and texts. To understand people's expectations of ritual effectiveness—how rituals are thought to work, or fail to work—I pay close attention to the distinct patterns people create as they articulate signs and texts in performance. I call this approach counterintuitive because motion implies dynamism, transgression, and transformation—seemingly the opposite of patterns' regularity. But patterns of ritual textuality are not static: they are continually created and reshaped in interactions between performers and audiences.

In observing the dynamism of patterns, I describe rituals as acts of *entextualization*, which is the process of turning discourse into texts that are detachable from their original contexts. In entextualization, discourse is made into "a unit—a text—that can be lifted out of its interactional setting" (Bauman and Briggs 1990: 73) and thereby made "replicable," able to be reproduced in new contexts (Urban 1996). As I demonstrate in the following chapters, the creation and replication of semiotic and textual objects in ritual performance often occur in regularly patterned ways. During my research on Christianity and politics in Fiji, I have observed how four basic patterns feature prominently: sequence, conjunction, contrast, and substitution. Each of the following chapters focuses on one of these types of pattern, and in the concluding chapter I consider variations within these types.

In the course of examining how ritual textuality works, I offer a portrait of contemporary social life in indigenous Fiji. As a Pentecostal pastor told the anthropologist Jacqueline Ryle in the late 1990s, "Fiji is very young and too old at the same time" (Ryle 2010: 130). By "very young," he meant that the nation, which became independent from Great Britain in 1970, is still being developed and is self-consciously behind other societies, not fully modern. By "too old," he meant that many indigenous Fijians venerate the past, treating it as the model of an ideal traditional order. But both past and present have come unstuck since 1987, when Fiji suffered the first of its four coups d'état. As the government's problems have worsened since then, the dominant Methodist Church has lost a significant proportion of its membership and the national council of chiefs has been deposed by a military-led regime aiming to establish itself as the foundation of a secure state. Although the social fabric has not quite been shredded, some of the thicker strands are being unraveled. Against this background, the following chapters highlight features of contemporary Fijian life including the new pulse of Pentecostalism, the social saturation of the beverage kava, and the snorting aggression of the military-led government. Taken together, they show the workings of ritual in a place humming with vigorous public discourse on political instability, religious pluralism, ethnic tensions, and overarching themes of the value of tradition and the vexation of its loss.

Ritual Textuality

In writing of "ritual textuality," I am deliberately not elevating "ritual" to the status of a thing to be isolated and dissected. Rather, I am treating ritual as a practical tendency—specifically, as entextualization—and analyzing it in terms of the connections people make between an event's semiotic and textual properties and ideologies of how those properties indicate that ritual actions are effective or ineffective. In approaching ritual this way, I am influenced by scholars such as Keane (1997, 2003, 2007), Robbins (2001a, 2001b), Silverstein (1992, 2004), and Stasch (2011), who have paid close attention to semiosis and semiotic ideologies in processes of ritualization, and those such as Tambiah (1985), Schieffelin (1985, 1996), and Rappaport (1999), who have emphasized ritual's performative aspects. In approaching "text" this way, I am drawing on Bakhtin, who defined text as "any coherent complex of signs," and developing Hanks's point that textuality "must be seen. . . as an instrument, a product, and a mode of social action" (Bakhtin 1986: 103; Hanks 1989: 103; see also Barber 2007).

The reason I write of ritual textuality in terms of pattern and motion is that people often look for, and try to create, particular kinds of patterns and motion in performance. For example, consider Simon Coleman's description of a failed Pentecostal service in late-1980s Sweden. During the sermon, preacher Svante Rumar posed a question to his audience: "Have we ever noticed the difference between a stillness that is empty and one that is full of God?" The question was a challenging one because for many Pentecostals, including the congregation listening to Rumar, stillness is the opposite of what one tries to achieve during worship. To become inspired by the Holy Spirit, the faithful should shout, dance, sing, and salute the sky with upraised hands. So why ask about stillness?

Coleman reports:

Rumar's words take on extra significance at the end of the service, when something unusual occurs. Normally, a sermon concludes with altar calls for conversion and healing, during which time the hall is filled with a cacophony of prayer, tongues and music. On this occasion, however, after a period of healing, the noise of the piano dies down. Rumar stands by the lectern, Bible in hand, as if poised to leave. But he doesn't move, and instead stands perfectly still and stares out into the middle distance. Silence falls.

I suspect that I am not the only person to sense the drama of the occasion but also the tension and even embarrassment evident within a congregation that had previously seemed upbeat but relaxed. After a few minutes, some people start to file out of the hall, and close to ten o'clock Rumar himself strides out of the service, without a word. After a few more minutes and many more exits there are just thirty to forty people still sitting in silence in their seats.

What had just happened? To this day, I am not quite sure. (Coleman 2006: 40)

Coleman, admirably, does not force an interpretation on his readers. For all we know, those thirty to forty people left sitting in the hall found the experience to be positive and intensely valuable, a ritual moment that changed their lives forever. Yet Coleman's account makes it clear that most of the audience found the experience uncomfortable, even distressing; they left the service before it was over, which is "an action explicitly frowned upon in the group" (2006: 40). By walking out, the audience seems to have indicated that this was not just a badly run service, but a failed one. It didn't work.

It didn't work because, as already noted, services are supposed to be lively, not still; loud, not silent. But there must be a greater reason than this for so many people to have left the service early, and Coleman suggests an especially intriguing possibility: Rumar was such a *good* model of appropriate Pentecostal activity that his anti-performance was powerful, not weak. As Coleman observes, Rumar did what Pentecostals are supposed to do. They speak about the power of words and then embody those words, turning promise into practice. But Rumar, acting in the right way, did the wrong thing: "he noted the power of stillness, and then he *became* stillness" (2006: 40).

How might describing ritual textuality in terms of pattern and motion help us to better understand Rumar's failure? On one level, Swedish Pentecostal services are completely overloaded with motion—physical motion, the movement of exuberant worshipers. On another level, an ideological one, people expect this motion to be both a cause and a sign of God's active presence. As Coleman writes elsewhere, the organization where he conducted fieldwork publishes "newsletters and magazines of well-known preachers, both Swedish and foreign, women as well as men, frozen in attitudes of motion as they speak and embody the Word of God" (2000: 148). By stopping motion, Rumar logically stopped God from entering the service, and people's lives and bodies. But he did so by following the proper pattern of Pentecostal worship, in which a person becomes the sign that he or she has described, embodying the model of ritual success. Rumar's experiment failed, then, because in terms of Pentecostal expectations of pattern and motion, it fit the pattern but stopped the motion. Rumar became a sign of stillness—but God is not still, so people should not be still, either.

Coleman's example is gripping because Pentecostals care so much about literal, physical movement. Indeed, it makes little sense to discuss Pentecostalism without analyzing the ways people and things bounce around, and in Chapter 2 I discuss the relationship between literal and metaphorical motion as I analyze a Pentecostal "crusade" in Suva. In the other chapters, however, the motion I analyze is primarily metaphorical, a representation of the idea that signs and texts figuratively *go places*—among themselves, against each other, and from person to person. In the analytical framework of this book, then, pattern is in motion and motion is manifest in pattern, so the two terms are not neatly separable.

In this regard, it is crucial to understand that ideas about pattern and motion are part of semiotic ideology more broadly: people's beliefs about what signs are in the first place, how they are thought to function, how they are thought to articulate with the "real" (nonsymbolic) world, and what effects their usage in ritual performance will have (Keane 1997, 2003, 2007; Silverstein 1992, 2004). What counts as motion will not be agreed upon by all people. For example, from the perspective of a European language speaker, it might seem obvious that one way a text "moves" is in its transmission through time; it had to get from yesterday to today somehow. Yet as Benjamin Whorf pointed out decades ago, a European language speaker's sense of time as something with physical properties—he compared it to "a row of bottles," "a ribbon or scroll marked off into equal blank spaces," and "an evenly scaled limitless tape measure"—derives from specific processes of grammatical and conceptual objectification of abstract entities (1956: 140, 153, 154). Given a different grammar and correspondingly different conception of time, European language speakers might not be inclined to characterize it in terms of motion as something that stretches before us, passes by us, and then vanishes.

As another example, consider the recent work of Patrick Eisenlohr (2010), who discusses why Muslims in Mauritius have so enthusiastically embraced the use of cassette tapes and compact discs to play recorded praise poetry (*na't*). Audio recordings are considered superior to books because they capture the immediacy and emotion of performance and ensure reliable transmission from authoritative reciters to their listeners. (He notes that "recordings from South Asia or those of local performers trained by Imams from India or Pakistan" are considered especially authoritative; 2010: 318.) As one young man explained, recordings present the voice of a reciter "in perfection. It is as if you were actually present when he is reading *na't*, it is almost like the entire emotional experience of being there.... It is a more direct way to learn about *na't* [than reading books], and to be touched by it" (2010: 327). The ideology of textual motion at work here, which draws on broader Islamic ideologies of divine communication, might be phrased like this: transmission from a perfect source is liable to corruption, and great care must be taken for the original text (revelation, composition, utterance, etc.) to get from its source to its audience without any changes; a chain of authoritative reciters can transmit the performance, but audio recordings more reliably reproduce all of the aspects of the original performance, and shorten the number of steps in transmission. Or, to put it bluntly: to experience divinity, you need unimpeded movement of a holy text from the author to yourself.

Putting Patterns into Motion

The first pattern I analyze in this book is one I call a *performative path*, a sequence whose interconnections are designed to make rituals effective. I use the term "performative" in the sense developed by J. L. Austin (1975) in his classic lectures on speech act theory. Performative utterances accomplish what they denote. For example, "I find you guilty," spoken under the right conditions—by a judge, in a courtroom, when a trial is taking place—makes you legally guilty. Saying "praise God" is actually to praise God and not merely describe the act of doing so. Rather than focus on the performativity of single utterances, I focus on the performativity of articulation: the ways that connections between rhetorical forms are meant to create connections between people and God. I call these kinds of articulation "paths" because a path is a channel for motion, a unit in itself but also a series of steps that goes somewhere and can be repeated (Parmentier 1987: 109).[2]

A good example of a performative path is a group of rituals performed by the Weyewa of Sumba, Indonesia, to address misfortune and restore good relations with ancestors. Joel Kuipers (1992) observes that over the course of these ceremonies, Weyewa mediums shift their patterns of speech to create the impression of disordered individual agents coming together into orderly solidarity. During sessions held to discover the source of a problem, diviners use a great deal of reported speech from the spirits that "suggests an image of dialogue in which participants are not in a state of consensus" (Kuipers 1992: 95). They frequently use verbs that Kuipers calls "locutives," which "frame an utterance as directly reported speech" (1992: 94). After the divination session comes a much longer ritual of placation in which orators use fewer locutives, and use them to quote other humans' speech rather than spirits' speech. Moreover, spirits' speech is now generally credited to "a distant ancestral spirit shared by all" (1992: 97). A third and final type of ceremony, meant to move from atonement to fulfilment, is sometimes held. In these rites, performers recite a myth in a "highly formalized" style, with no locutives or reported speech as shown in Kuipers's example. The performance is dominated by the use of distinctive formulaic couplets considered to be an inheritance from ancestral spirits (1992: 98–99). The articulations across the ceremonies—the ways in which many voices gradually become one—effectively model a movement from disorder to order, disagreement to agreement, and division to unity.

The second pattern I examine, *chiasmus*, is a kind of conjunction. It is "criss-cross reciprocation" (Silverstein 2004: 626), or an "X-shaped" relationship between signs. Chiasmus is a prominent literary feature that can be as simple as Shakespeare's evocative lament of Richard II, "I wasted time, and now doth time waste me" (Richard II, 5.5), which follows a simple A–B–B'–A' pattern, or as complex as the "precise, extensive, and elegant" chiasmus of Psalm 3:6–8, which follows a pattern of A–B–C–D–E–F–F'–E'–D'–C'–B'–A' (Welch 1981b: 10). Indeed, entire works can be structured chiastically, as John W. Welch argues for the Book of Revelation (Welch 1981a).

For chiasmus as a ritual pattern, Michael Silverstein offers the especially lucid example of Christian communion. In communion, "our symbolic incorporation (eating and drinking) of Christ's transubstantiated 'Body and Blood' ritually results, contrariwise, in our *being* incorporated *into* His body and blood made corporate on earth, the fellowship and institution of the church" (2003: 33–34; emphasis in original). In other words, in the act of consuming bread and wine, a person symbolically takes Christ into himself or herself, and in doing so, puts himself or herself into Christ, understood as the body of the Christian Church. (Bodily metaphors of Church and Christ are found in biblical passages such as 1 Corinthians 12:12–27 and Colossians 1:18.) The X-shaped relationship ritually conjoins person and institution, past and present, and immanence and transcendence.

The third pattern I analyze is *fractal recursivity*, which involves contrast rather than sequence or conjunction. It is a relationship between two opposed categories that can be subdivided repeatedly, forming an overall structure of nested homologies. As Susan Gal observes, "To be fractal, a distinction must be co-constitutive, so that the terms—like *right* and *left* or *east* and *west*—define each other....[W]hatever the local, historically specific cultural prototypes or images that motivate [such] oppositions...the distinction can be reproduced repeatedly by projecting it onto narrower and broader comparisons" (2005: 26–27; emphases in original). The categories of *life* and *death* are a vivid example of a fractally recursive pair. They might seem to be stark opposites—one is either alive or dead—but in fact the categories are not neatly opposed. Within "life" is a division between the "living alive," such as all of us who are currently thinking and moving, and the "living [but] dead," such as those in comas and those imprisoned on death row waiting to be executed. Within the category of "death" exist the "dead dead," those who are gone and forgotten, and the "dead [but] living," such as ghosts, vampires, zombies, and ancestors who play significant roles in the affairs of their descendants. These subcategories can be divided, too; some of the living dead are a lot more alive than others. Because life and death are fractally recursive categories, acts of defining them in absolute terms are attempts at gatekeeping and therefore claims to authority. For example, judicial debates in the United States over boundaries between life and death show how fractally recursive categories mark out zones of political contest. In 1876, the Hawaiian legislature passed a bill that declared lepers to be "dead, and considered alike with those in tombs" (Osorio 2002: 178), and in 2005 congressional representatives rushed to Washington, DC, to legislate the life of Terri Schiavo, a woman who had been in a coma for a decade and a half.

Finally, the fourth pattern I examine is *monologue*, or speaking in the singular voice of substitution. Monologue is meant to substitute for other voices and texts and to preclude the possibility of meaningful response. It features prominently in religious and political discourse, but has been under-analyzed by scholars. Bakhtin suggested that monologic projects gained force especially during the Enlightenment: "Even when one is dealing with a collective, with a multiplicity of creating forces," he wrote, "unity is nevertheless illustrated through the image of a single conscious-ness: the spirit of a nation, the spirit of a people, the spirit of history, and so forth. Everything capable of meaning can be gathered together in one consciousness and subordinated to a unified accent" (1984: 82). The key word is "subordinated": in monologue, as I am using the term, elements are brought together in erasure and replacement—the logic of substitu-tion—rather than complementarity. Monologue is a kind of overwriting, a two-part pattern in which one text is meant to get rid of another.

A spectacular example of monologue comes from the quotations of Mao Zedong, especially from his Little Red Book, which Chinese citi-zens were required to carry and recite during the Cultural Revolution. In the mid-1960s, workers were obligated to meet several times weekly to discuss Mao's sayings, especially as they related to ongoing projects. Eventually, however, "connection with the daily work became attenuated. Workers were expected to memorize three new Mao-sayings for each study session, and considerable time was spent simply going around the group listening to the recitations and drilling those who had not done their homework" (Whyte 1974: 176). Memorization could become an end in itself: one memoirist recalls a woman who "recited all 270 pages of the red book without missing a word" (Gao 1987: 318). Besides being read in study sessions, Mao's quotations blazed from billboards and blared from loudspeakers (Gao 1987: 163; Chang 2004: 368). The political prisoner Nien Cheng recalled in her memoir:

> New guards came to work wearing the red armbands of the Revolutionaries. Early in the morning, at midday and at night, I would hear them shouting to each other "Long Live Our Great Leader Chairman Mao" and chanting his quotations. The newspa-per reported a new ritual observed by all Chinese people called, "Ask for instructions in the mornings, check your action with Chairman Mao's teachings at noon and report everything at night." Apparently everyone went through the formality in front of an official portrait of Mao. To ask for instructions was to read passages from the Little Red Book, to check was to read again from the same book and to report was also to read from the same book. (Cheng 1986: 169)

Mao's quotations were thus a model for both exerting authority and sub-mitting to it. This model was ever-expansive, and "a movement to 'revo-lutionize daily life'...consisted of replacing daily talk with quotations from Chairman Mao. When you got out of bed in the morning, instead of saying, 'Let's get up,' you said, 'Carry the revolution through to the end.' When you went to bed, you said, 'Never forget class struggle'" (Gao 1987: 318–319). The motion of monologue, in Maoist China, was torrential. With such intense, ritualized attention to Mao's words, the books themselves became magical tokens, fetishized objects of power (Zuo 1991).

The four patterns I have described are formally distinct. They can intersect, however, because entextualization is an interactive and ongoing process, not a single closed-off act. For example, Christian communion is not only a strong example of chiasmus but it is also a performative path in which participants enact the narrative of the Last Supper. Moreover, the shifting boundaries between divinity and humanity in Christ, the celebrant, and the communicants trace fractally recursive relationships in which divine and human interpenetrate. And when communion is conducted in a mission field as a way of marking particular community members as newly authorized and spiritually privileged, it can also function as a kind of monologue, shouting down and drowning out alternative ritual practices. The signs and texts that move in ritual performances can be multiply patterned, then, but their basic patterns can be distinguished as one traces their complex articulations.

I emphasize that typology itself is not the point of this book. The types I have listed are neither definitive nor complete, and they do not explain anything in themselves. Ritual performances are not automatically judged to be effective if they simply follow a recognizable textual pattern. Ritual participants always need to confront matters of what Bakhtin called addressivity, the dialogic "quality of being directed to someone" (1986: 95): who is the event for, and what are the limits of participation? But patterns do emerge in performance, and, as I show in the following chapters, are framed by participants' semiotic ideologies and their understandings of Christian subjectivity and divine and human agency. It may seem that patterns set social life in stone, and as Asif Agha notes wryly, "when it comes to culture, taxonomy is taxidermy" (2007: 2). I am arguing, however, that patterns emerge interactively in performance and are best understood in terms of transformation, not stasis.[3] This is why I use the metaphor of motion, even as I am wary of how routinely it is now used in anthropology.

Fijian Ground

The following chapters move between two fieldsites: the villages of Tavuki Bay on the rural island of Kadavu, and the national capital, Suva. Kadavu is located in Fiji's south and is the nation's fourth largest island (see Figures 1.1 and 1.2). It has a population of 10,000, nearly all of whom are indigenous Fijians. Many of the villagers in Tavuki Bay work as farmers and fishers, with some entrepreneurs and government employees. Suva, a six-hour boat trip or half-hour plane ride from Kadavu, sits in the southeast corner of Vitilevu, Fiji's largest island (see Figure 1.3). The city has a

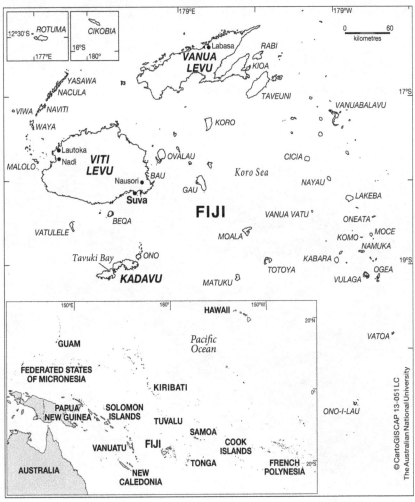

FIGURE 1.1 Map of Fiji. ©The Australian National University, CAP CartoGIS.

FIGURE I.2 Tavuki village, Kadavu, 2006.

FIGURE I.3 Suva, 2009.

multiethnic population of 85,000, and the Suva–Nausori "corridor" has more than 240,000 residents (Fiji Islands Bureau of Statistics 2007). By keeping village and city together in the same analytical frame, I intend to talk about stability and change without implying that stability is found only in villages and change is found only in cities.

To describe Kadavu evocatively, one should begin at a meal, a kava-drinking session, or a church service. Christina Toren writes that during her most recent research in another rural island, she "came to the conclusion that food is the key to everything Fijian. It figures powerfully, not only in kinship relations, but in... ritualized formalities of attendance on one another" by different clans (2009: 132). Food in Fiji is a sign of others' care for you: if you are thin, it reflects badly on your family (Becker 1995). And so, in Kadavu, your belly is stuffed, and then stuffed some more, with starchy crops like taro, cassava, sweet potatoes, yams, and breadfruit, with plenty of fish, prawns, crabs, and, on special occasions, pork. Purchased foods include rice, instant noodles, chicken, and tinned mackerel, tuna, and beef. Rounding out the rounded diet are locally grown coconuts, mangoes, Tahitian chestnuts, citrus fruits, taro leaves, guavas, eggplants, pumpkins, and chili peppers. The most popular item to consume is not food, however, but kava, a beverage made from the dried and crushed roots and stems of a plant of the same name. Most adult men drink kava every day, usually in the evenings, in casual group sessions. Many women drink, too.

A sensory overload—the pleasant crush of food, the flood of kava, the acrid smoke of cooking fires and cigarettes—spills into the whorl of green and blue that is Kadavu's landscape and seascape. Everything moves through a social network vibrating in constant connection, a nexus of kin relations, emplaced memories, and, articulating it all, a hushed respect for chiefly authority coupled with deep anxiety at the perceived loss of indigenous power. This sense of loss, I have argued elsewhere, is generated by interactions between the chiefly system and Christianity (Tomlinson 2009). More than 99 percent of Kadavu's residents are Christians, and more than 80 percent belong to the Methodist Church (Fiji Islands Bureau of Statistics 2007).

The island has significant economic potential, although there is little infrastructure, with limited electricity in many places, a drinking water supply that is not always reliable, and few roads. Farmers hope that kava will become a lucrative cash crop internationally, especially as it is turned into pills to relieve stressed-out Westerners. Unfortunately, the international market price plunged in the late 1990s due to a scare over kava's effect on the liver. Moreover, Fiji's citizens drink so much kava that they do not yet grow enough for the domestic market and import extra supplies from Vanuatu. Tourism has strong potential if the global economy is healthy and the national political situation becomes calm. The Great Astrolabe Reef arcs around Kadavu's eastern and southern edges, dotted with small-scale diving resorts taking advantage of the spectacular coral formations to which scuba divers have given names like Featherstar, Evil Trench, and Crazy Maze.[4]

Many people from Kadavu migrate to Suva for its economic and educational opportunities. Suva has a sloppy energy, a ragged grace: the pavement sweats grit and cigarette butts, and the humidity sinks into your pores like lead, but the city stretches in its own skin. Several popular authors have sketched Suva vividly. Ngaio Marsh describes Inspector Alleyn standing on the deck of a ship as it pulls away from the Suva wharf: "The smell must not be forgotten—frangipanni, coco-nut oil, and sodden wood.... The darkness of everything and the violence of colour—it was a pattern of wet brown, acid green, magenta and indigo" (Marsh 1997: 1–2). Paul Theroux quotes an expatriate Canadian in the city who said, "Suva reminds me of an aunt of mine who drank too much.... She was delightful. But she was prone to stumble. Her clothes were a little askew, and there was always a strap of her slip showing" (Theroux 1992: 229). Perhaps the most evocative passage comes from the anthropologist Buell Quain, who conveyed Suva's aura, as seen by indigenous Fijians, of newness, excitement, and risk. He called the city

> that hilarious fleshpot of the Pacific, which is the source of songs built on new harmonies, tales of happy drunken brawls, and vices too delicate for all but the seasoned epicure. Opportunity was there, a whole new vista, open for him who chose to learn these new delights. One girl had been to Suva and came back [to rural Vanualevu] dancing the Charleston. A new life, not well understood but withal cheerful, had supplanted the old. (Quain 1948: 1)

Despite the violence of coups, Suva keeps growing. Each time I have returned since 1996, there have been several fresh new buildings gleaming with the promise of prosperity—but that promise does not always filter down to street level. There are many squatter settlements located between the city and the town of Nausori, and even with some economic recovery in the late 2000s, the percentage of Fiji's total population in poverty stands above 30 percent, with rural poverty rates increasing during the decade to more than 40 percent (Narsey, Raikoti, and Waqavonovono 2010).

Because businesses owned by Indo-Fijians (citizens of Indian descent) are so prominent in Suva, the indigenous paramount chief and nation's first prime minister, Ratu Sir Kamisese Mara, once commented sarcastically that "if Suva were burned down, the [indigenous] Fijians would lose nothing except the record of their debts" (1997: 65). Most Indo-Fijians are the descendants of laborers who came to Fiji between 1879 and 1916 to work on sugarcane plantations. Approximately 80 percent of the immigrants came from Uttar Pradesh, 13 percent came from Bihar and Bengal, and a smaller percentage came from other parts of India including Gujarat (Srebrnik 2002: 192; see also Kelly 1991; Lal 1992: 39). Discord between Indo-Fijians and indigenous Fijians is expressed in many ways and helped motivate indigenous support for coups in 1987 and 2000. Because of the coups, as many as 120,000 Indo-Fijians have emigrated (Lal 2011: 65–66, 156), lowering their proportion of the national population from approximately one half to one third. As of 2007, indigenous Fijians comprised almost 57 percent of the population (Fiji Bureau of Statistics 2007). One of the key markers of difference between the two communities is religious identity: Indo-Fijians are largely Hindus and Muslims, whereas nearly all indigenous Fijians are Christians.

Christianity has a vibrant public presence throughout Fiji, and many churches are notably large, well-kept, impressive buildings (see Figures 1.4, 1.5, 1.6, and 1.7). At secular public events, church ministers are often invited to provide opening and closing prayers. In the Tavuki Bay area, villagers are drawn together by Methodist projects such as raising funds and putting on feasts for church events, as well as sending their children to the church-run high school at Rijimodi (Richmond). In Suva, no church dominates—indeed, no religion dominates, because Suva is multicultural, multiethnic, multifaith, multi-everything. Aggressive Christian evangelists tend to take over public spaces like parks, however, and one often sees posters and banners for their crusades. Religious enthusiasm spills onto the pages of the daily newspapers, whose editorial sections are treated by letter writers like religious blogs, spaces in which they speak about subjects such as the identity of the true God and true religion, the holiness of the Sabbath, whether baptism should be conducted for infants or adults, and signs of the end times. A notably enthusiastic correspondent,

FIGURE 1.4 Methodist church, Tavuki, 2010.

Dr. Tobey Huff, once managed to squeeze sixty-seven separate Bible references into a single letter to the editor.[5]

Plan of the Book

Each of the following chapters focuses on one of the patterns I have
described previously, beginning with the discussion in Chapter 2 of performative paths. Performative paths are sequences in which the articulation of elements gives rituals their perceived effectiveness. In the event
I analyze, a Pentecostal service in Suva led by an evangelist from Texas,
the sequence is also a loop: the preacher keeps shaping the same pattern as he moves repeatedly in his rhetoric from declarations to promises
to actions. I have chosen to begin with this particular case study for two
reasons. First, scholarship on Fiji generally falls into two camps: one cen-
tered on indigenous Fijians and the other on Indo-Fijians. Scholars are
increasingly attempting to avoid this polarization, however, and by beginning with this event I am attempting to treat Fijian public space as neither inherently nor exclusively indigenous nor Indian. I want to begin, in
short, by strategically avoiding the discourse of ethnicity in Fiji while not
denying that it remains politically volatile. Second, the texts I analyze—the

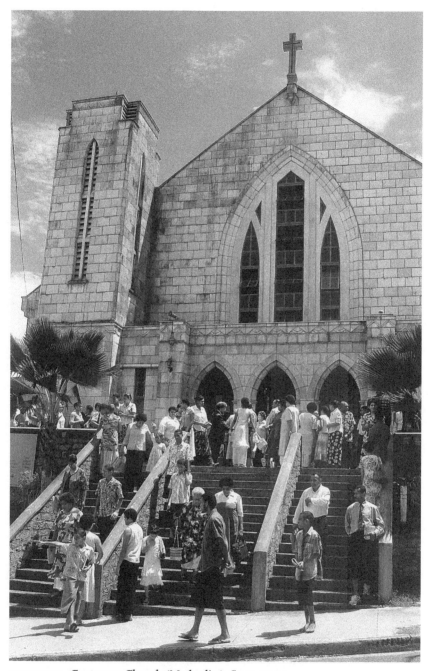

FIGURE 1.5 Centenary Church (Methodist), Suva, 2009.

FIGURE 1.6   Sacred Heart Cathedral (Catholic), Suva, 2009.

FIGURE I.7 World Harvest Centre (Christian Mission Fellowship), Suva, 2010.

Pentecostal sermon and altar call—are flamboyantly appealing. Brother Kenneth Colegrove's piquant language, sense of urgency, and artful use of parallelism make the texts enjoyable to read as an extended poem on themes of divinity, faith, and motion.

In Chapter 3, I analyze chiasmus, the conjunction of counterposed elements. As mentioned, Christian communion is a good example of chiasmus: when communicants take Christ into themselves, they put themselves into Christ. I argue that Fijian kava-drinking sessions follow this same X-shaped pattern but do so in relation to the *vanua* (land, people, and chiefdoms). When people drink kava, they are taking the *vanua* into themselves and likewise—or rather, crosswise—putting themselves into the *vanua*. This pattern helps explain why many Fijian Methodists find the idea of using kava instead of wine in communion to be deeply problematic: maintaining a boundary between Christian communion and kava drinking is a vital project because people recognize that their patterns of entextualization run parallel to each other and *could* be merged.

In Chapter 4 I describe fractal recursivity, the pattern of contrast involving two terms whose distinction is co-constitutive. The sets of terms I examine are (1) life and death and (2) private and public. The chapter's historical focus is Methodist missionaries' accounts of "happy deaths," nineteenth-century scenes in which dying Fijians said and did the "right" things to indicate they were going to heaven. Missionaries published stories of happy deaths in reports and magazines, creating a reading public whose members could participate vicariously in the creation of global Christendom. I argue that by redrawing textual boundaries between life/death and private/public, the missionaries created a new demonic private sphere, which I discuss with reference to disturbing stories from Kadavu in 2003 that were tied to the death of a high chief.

Finally, Chapter 5 is about monologue. I draw on mass-media material gathered since Fiji's coup of December 2006 to show how the military-led government promotes its own discursive projects while attempting to silence opponents through intimidation and censorship. It is a brutal form of substitution and can be visualized as a straight line that erases all before it and brooks no deviation. In Fiji, this brutality serves an aggressive utopian project in which coup leader-turned-prime minister Voreqe Bainimarama suggests that if everyone says the same thing, the nation will move forward in united progress. Monologue is his ongoing, ritualized effort: like a Weyewa orator, Bainimarama wants to unite every voice. But rather than do so through a path of careful articulations, he does it in an abrupt, militaristic way that has not been especially successful.

All of the chapters treat ritual in terms of entextualization, but they also resonate with other, well-established scholarly understandings of ritual. For example, the Pentecostal crusade discussed in Chapter 2 exemplifies Tambiah's description of a ritual "logic of persuasion" in which "redundant patterns fuse into one configurational totality, one cumulative experience, one superimposition of successive sequences" (Tambiah 1985 [1979]: 151, 153; emphasis deleted). Chapters 3 and 4 feature events that most anthropologists would recognize as classic rituals, each with its own quirks. Kava-drinking sessions are forms of communion, but they are not always reverential, and because of kava's connection to ancestral spirits, kava drinking has an aura of risk, unlike the Eucharist. Deathbed scenes are rites of passage in which the liminal subjects serve as eyewitnesses to the invisible and announce their forthcoming success, but can achieve it only by dying. The chapter on monologue, describing the self-appointed prime minister's attempts to reshape government and society in his own militaristic image, illustrates David Kertzer's pithy claim that "rite makes might" (Kertzer 1988). Bainimarama is ultimately engaged in ritualization as an "act...of power in the fashioning of structures" (Kelly and Kaplan 1990: 140).

In this book, I use the metaphor of motion to apprehend the dynamism of interactively created patterns of ritual textuality. I also show the ways in which participants shape their practices according to their own senses of the characteristics and consequences of different kinds of motion, both literal and metaphorical. The goal of the Pentecostal crusade was to create exuberant Christian subjects who were sure that God had forgiven them of their sins, and physical motion was the key: audience members were urged to stand, clap, and shout their way to salvation. The analysis of kava-drinking sessions as rituals of communion hinges on the double meaning of the Fijian term *vanua*: it is both place and people, with the former immobile and the latter mobile. The missionaries who published stories of happy deaths were trying, among other things, to replace the traditional narrative of the Fijian afterlife with their own new story, one in which a soul no longer faced a difficult journey fighting off monsters but passed painlessly to heaven. As this new story became established, the ancestral spirits were displaced but not erased, and they still move about the landscape. Finally, the motion that Bainimarama seeks is progress: the transformation of society as it moves toward a bigger, better, faster future.

To say that signs and texts, or culture more broadly, can "move" is a useful starting point for scholars. But to avoid making sociocultural processes seem automatic, it is crucial to be clear about what one means by motion. Metaphors must remain in our analytical sights as metaphors, with scholars reflecting on the insights they provide while acknowledging their limitations (Rumsey 2004). By analyzing basic patterns of entextualization—sequence, conjunction, contrast, and substitution—in terms of motion, I hope to prompt new thinking about ritual textuality, especially the ways people shape their own expectations and evaluations of what counts as an effective ritual performance.

2

The Holy Ghost Is About to Fall

DECEMBER 4, 2008, is a muggy night in Suva. I am walking toward the city from the neighborhood of Veiuto, at the tip of Suva's peninsula, and the scents of wet earth, blossoms, and bus exhaust anoint the air with their peculiar blessings. A modern garden blooms on the foreshore, the mud festooned at low tide with plastic and Styrofoam, glass bottles and aluminum cans, and crowned with the arches of half-sunken car tires. The water in the harbor is dead calm, but mountains surge on the horizon.

I'm heading for a Pentecostal rally in Albert Park, part of a weeklong "crusade" being held by the United Pentecostal Church International (UPCI) of Fiji. Albert Park, where the flag of the independent nation of Fiji was first raised on October 10, 1970, is a parade ground for Fiji's ghosts. Nearby, on the site of the national museum, is where the area's original village stood until its residents were relocated by the colonial government; next to the park, at the government complex, independent Fiji suffered its first coup in 1987. The crusade is taking place in the corner of the park nearest downtown Suva and the sea, on a large rectangle of dirt and grass with the main stage on one side facing the grandstand on the other. The main stage is really two platforms, one for the service leaders and one for the choir. Flanking the open space in the middle are long rows of benches under temporary roofs of corrugated iron.

As I arrive, the choir is already singing and swaying, accompanied by buoyant keyboards, guitar, and drums. I sit high in the park's grandstand to get a good overview and, I confess, to minimize the chance that I will be yanked into a place of ritual prominence. Before long, an energetic crowd has arrived, probably more than a thousand people in all. Most of them are indigenous Fijians, including many children and young adults as well as middle-aged worshipers. As the crowd grows, so does the energy. Soon the central worship space is rushed by people in constant motion. Children dart into it, running in delight. Adults whirl small towels, clap, and thrust their hands toward heaven.

This is completely different from my original subject of research, Fijian Methodism, whose services are calm and tightly coordinated. Fijian Methodist services feature stately a capella hymns, formal oratory from chiefs and church officials, and elegant prayers studded with honorific references to God. This raucous Pentecostal affair, by contrast, is an explosion—a riot. I'm waiting for the sermon, because I have studied Methodist sermons and this seems like a promising point of comparison. But the longer I sit—realizing that I'm not supposed to be sitting, I'm supposed to be dancing—the more I come to realize that talk itself isn't the point of this event. Motion is.

By now, people have been swaying, jumping, whirling, and whooping for more than an hour, using the choir as a musical drive toward spiritual ecstasy. People are caught up in each moment, thrust forward to a succession of peaks. The worshipers seem tireless, their bodies like waves that keep cresting but never crash (Figure 2.1). As the momentum continues to build, I begin to wonder: what can a sermon possibly achieve in this context? If a Fijian Methodist preacher were to stand up and begin expostulating on a point of doctrine here, it would be verbal morphine, numbing and dulling the intensity.

FIGURE 2.1 Pentecostal crusade in Albert Park, Suva, 2008.

The preacher is finally introduced as "Brother Kenneth Colegrove, from Texas." As he begins to speak, it becomes clear that his sermon is meant to excite people the same way the music and dancing does. He doesn't want to drain energy from the park. He wants to overload the circuits. "Thank you Brother Reid, praise the Lord everybody. Why don't you stand on your feet and put your hands together, clap your hands and magnify Jesus!" From these opening lines, Colegrove wants people to move: to stand, to clap, to worship with every sinew. And the crowd is with him, yelling "yes!" as he sustains intensity from the very beginning:

He is King of Kings and Lord of Lords! He is omnipotent! He is almighty. He is all-powerful. Everything is in His hands. He is our healer. I said Jesus is our healer. Jesus is our deliverer. Jesus is our very present help in the time of trouble. There is nothing that he cannot do. There is no power of Satan that he cannot destroy. There is no disease that he cannot heal. There is no sickness that he can [not] set free from. There is no wounded, broken, twisted soul or spirit that Jesus cannot set free. He said "Behold, all power is given to me in heaven and in earth." Come on, who will believe here tonight? Where's those that will believe? Where are those that will have faith? Come let us lift our hands and magnify Jesus. Praise God. Praise God, feel the Holy Ghost here.

For the next twenty-five minutes, Colegrove exhorts people to get ready for the Holy Ghost to arrive. This is a sermon that dances between exclamation marks. It is designed to make people act—not in the general sense of being good Christians but in the specific sense of being ecstatic Christians, and not in the hazy realm of future days but in the sharply focused present.

The Holy Ghost (or Holy Spirit; *Yalo Tabu* in Fijian) is part of Christianity's godhead along with God the father and Jesus the son. In Pentecostal doctrine, the Holy Ghost is the divine figure that "can fill earthly people with God's heavenly power in order to allow them, among other things, to speak in tongues, heal, speak prophetically, lead moral lives, and bring others to the faith" (Robbins 2009: 62). The United Pentecostal Church International, based in Hazelwood, Missouri, is distinct from many other Pentecostal churches for its emphasis on "Oneness," the unitarian nature of God, and UPCI members "prefer to refer to Father, Son and Spirit as 'modes' or 'manifestations' of God" rather than as "separate and distinct 'Persons'" (Anderson 2004: 50; see also Jacobsen 2003; Wacker 1984: 355). For Oneness Pentecostals, speaking in tongues (glossolalia) displays a "gift of the spirit" which is considered a requirement for salvation along with repentance and baptism (Anderson 2004: 50). Colegrove's preaching is meant to make people so excited that the Holy Ghost must "fall" on Albert Park, and his sermon links the opening hour of music to the altar call, during which people will be called up to the platform to repent and speak in tongues before they get baptized.

Declaration–Promise–Action

Colegrove's sermon makes his audience move physically. God is also expected to move, with the Holy Ghost falling from heaven and Jesus getting ready to walk through Albert Park: "Can I tell somebody here tonight that right here in Albert Park—a place that was built so that people could play games," Colegrove preaches at one point, "Jesus is gonna walk by, Jesus is gonna walk by, and he's not comin' to play games." But in a less obvious sense the sermon "moves" by the continual articulation of a sequence. Colegrove excites his audience by linking distinct kinds of speech acts in a consistent pattern which I refer to as *declaration-promise-action*. The articulation of the three parts in a figurative loop—declarations with promises, promises with actions, and actions with declarations—encourages the audience to craft a specific kind of spiritual subjectivity: a self that moves individually for God, and is moved individually by God.

Declaration-promise-action, then, is my shorthand term for this group of linked speech acts. The first category, "declaration," consists of declarative statements, such as "Where the Spirit of the Lord is, there is liberty." The second, "promise," includes statements about future events and hoped-for situations ("I tell you... the Holy Ghost is gonna be poured out in this place tonight"), beliefs ("I believe that the Holy Ghost can release me from the bondage of sin"), and questions ("Where are those that will pray with me right now?"), which can often function as indirect commands. The third category, "action," includes direct commands ("Lift up your voice to the Lord and somebody call on Him") as well as thanks, praise, verbal ejaculations such as "Hallelujah," and, twice during the sermon and then at the conclusion of the altar call, glossolalia.

Colegrove continually moves from the first category to the second, then the second to the third, and then back through the cycle again. The movement from first to second to third categories can be seen as an oscillation from past and present situations to future ones, and then back to the present. The "declaration" category features statements about past and present, whereas the "promise" category often provokes consideration of the future, whether by describing a hoped-for event, suggesting the implications of a belief, or posing a question. The "action" category then returns to the present. The beginning of Colegrove's sermon, quoted earlier, fits this pattern exactly. After opening with a string of declarations about who Jesus is and what he can do ("He is King of Kings and Lord of Lords!"), Colegrove poses short questions about the audience's belief and faith ("who will believe here tonight?"), and then issues a series of commands: "Come let us lift our hands and magnify Jesus. Praise God. Praise God, feel the Holy Ghost here."

The observation that rhetoric's persuasive force comes partly from its structure goes back to Aristotle (Kennedy 1991) and has seen complex elaborations, such as Rudolf Bultmann's analysis of how Paul paired seemingly contradictory indicatives and imperatives to argue "that what God has done is the basis of what justified believers must do" (Rosner 1995: 19). In addition, as Niko Besnier has observed, speaking performatively—that is, speaking in order to fit or shape the context in which one's words are judged forceful or effective—depends on sequences of previous usage: "What conditions the success of performative acts is the extent to which they invoke prior utterances and actions that carry authorizing legitimacy and reinforce the performativity of the current utterance" (2009: 166). The remarkable thing about Colegrove's performance, in this regard, is how it not only reaches back to the authoritative model of the Bible, but also continually reaches both backward and forward within itself as a surprisingly coherent and self-contained structure. That is, in cycling between declarations, promises, and actions, Colegrove lays the groundwork for his own performative authority and the audience's response to it. It is also crucial to note that the pattern of declaration-promise-action is found cross-culturally, as I describe later. I am not arguing, therefore, that Colegrove's approach is a novel one. It is, however, evidently an appealing and effective one.

The categories of declaration, promise, and action are ideal types, and some statements could be classified as more than one depending on whether one focuses on grammar or on pragmatic frames. For example, consider Colegrove's statement: "Ladies and gentlemen, it is God's will, it is His divine purpose, that you leave this place tonight filled with the baptism of the Holy Ghost." This is phrased as a declaration, but it points forward like a promise—you *will* be filled—and it comes close to functioning as an imperative: *be filled!* In addition, reported speech that is framed as declaration can include promises and commands, as when Colegrove preaches "Then Peter said unto them, 'repent and be baptized…' " When I quote Colegrove in the following examples, I label the categories that I have applied in analysis so that readers can observe my classifications.

A clear and compact example of the declaration-promise-action pattern comes immediately after the quoted excerpt. Having urged his audience to "feel the Holy Ghost here," Colegrove continues:

> [Declaration:] I feel the Holy Ghost here tonight. I feel the presence of the Lord in this place. Where the Spirit of the Lord is, there is liberty. [Promise:] You may have come here tonight bound, but you're gonna leave here free. You may have come tonight with chains hanging on you and the bondage of sin holding you in captivity, but there is a deliverer who is present in Albert Park tonight. [Action:] Thank you, Jesus.

In this excerpt, he begins with three straightforward declarations, then turns to two grammatically complex promises based on the assumption that his audience is morally broken and spiritually yearning: they are bound, but will be freed. Finally, he finishes with a simple utterance of thanks. Taken on its own, this is an artful piece of rhetoric. The preacher moves from simple sentence structures to complex ones and then back to simple ones, and he draws a triangle between himself, his audience, and Jesus. What is remarkable about the crusade of December 4, 2008, is that Colegrove's entire performance follows the declaration-promise-action pattern shown in this short excerpt.

Here are six additional examples demonstrating how Colegrove creates the three-part pattern in a continuously looping path. The first two examples come immediately after the one given previously:

> [Declaration:] The stage has been set. The atmosphere has been charged. Faith is in this place. [Promise:] And I believe—I wisht I could find someone else who will believe—I believe that God is going to do miracles here tonight.[1] I believe God is going to heal sick bodies tonight. I believe that God is going to fill people with the baptism of the Holy Ghost just like it happened in Acts chapter two. [Action:] Praise God, *haya-boko-taya-bahaya*, whoo! Praise God. Praise God, come on, clap your hands to the Lord again.

[Declaration:] I have a church back home in the heart of Texas that is praying for this crusade, that is praying for an outpouring of the Holy Ghost. [Promise:] Hey it might rain again tonight, but I tell you what else is gonna happen, the Holy Ghost is gonna be poured out in this place tonight. [Action:] Turn to somebody and tell 'em, "Get ready for it." Get ready for it. I said, get ready for it!

Both of these excerpts move crisply from declaration to promise to action. The first one is notable because Colegrove speaks in tongues. I have written it phonetically as *haya-boko-taya-bahaya*; he drops the phrase into the middle of his speech, showing that he is already inspired by the Holy Ghost. In the second excerpt, after alluding to the previous night's weather ("Hey it might rain again tonight") and drawing a parallel between rainfall and a deluge of divine presence, Colegrove commands his audience to speak: "Turn to somebody and tell 'em, 'Get ready for it.'" This is the first time he attempts to get his audience to repeat his words, or, more precisely, to create a transposition (Eisenlohr 2010; Shoaps 1999, 2002) in which they also carry his intentions and motivations forward into their own speech.

Colegrove sometimes develops the three-part pattern at greater length. Shortly after the excerpts quoted, he preaches:

[Declaration:] "To an inheritance incorruptible and undefiled, that fadeth not away, reserved in heaven for you: you are kept by the power of God, through faith, through faith, through faith, unto salvation, ready to be revealed in the last time." [Promise:] I'm preachin' about faith that brings salvation, faith that's gonna take you somewhere, faith that's gonna lead you to a lively hope, faith that's gonna turn your circumstance around. Faith that's going to turn your life upside down, faith that's going to destroy the power of sin in your life, faith that's going to give you deliverance through the name of Jesus. Where are those that will pray with me right now? [Action:] "God, send your Spirit down in this place tonight. Send the power of the Holy Ghost down in this place tonight. In the name of Jesus, in the name of Jesus, in the name of Jesus." Look at somebody standing next to you and ask them, "Have you ever received the baptism of the Holy Ghost?" If they said "no," then you start right now praying that before the service is over God is going to fill them with a marvelous, glorious, wonderful gift of the Holy Ghost.

This excerpt has several notable features. The declaration ("To an inheritance...") comes from 1 Peter 1:4–5. In quoting this text, Colegrove tries to keep the audience excited by repeating "through faith, through faith, through faith," his voice rising slightly in pitch the third time. (Some audience members shout in response.) In the promise segment, after listing the many things that faith will do, he concludes with a command masquerading as a question: "Where are those that will pray with me right now?" He then moves firmly into the action segment by telling people what words they should use in prayer—which are, notably, commands to God: the line "God, send your spirit down..." is a double command in which Colegrove tells people to tell God what to do. After this, Colegrove tells audience members how to speak to each other, instructing them to ask their neighbor if they have "received the baptism of the Holy Ghost." Anticipating a possible "no," he adds another command to pray.

A fourth example shows how even as Colegrove adapts his sermon to the context of performance, he sticks closely to the declaration-promise-action pattern. Immediately after the previously quoted section, he preaches:

[Declaration:] Hey it's still happenin', folks. There were people [who] received the Holy Ghost right here, last night, in the rain. [Promise:] I believe that we can see a hundred receive the Holy Ghost right here tonight. [Action:] Put your hands together, clap your hands again and magnify Jesus. Amen. [Declaration:] I don't know how you do it in Fiji, [Action:] if you have to be seated, be seated; if you wanna keep standin', keep standin', but let's let God do somethin' here tonight. Hallelujah. Hallelujah.

After mentioning the previous night's events, Colegrove anticipates new success tonight, setting a target of one hundred people to be saved. He follows with a string of commands, interrupted only by a quick declaration of his ignorance of local culture: "I don't know how you do it in Fiji." He tells his audience that whether they sit or stand, they need to be faithfully excited for God to come. Colegrove is reaching out to his audience, so to speak, by calling attention to the specific time and place they share. He does this to illustrate Christianity's global reach and to frame the various lessons he will deliver during the sermon and altar call (Tomlinson 2012a). Later on, he flatters them by declaring, "My Lord, I like the way y'all worship here in Fiji. I like the way you sing. I like the way you give God the praise."

Colegrove uses negative terms to spur his listeners into recognizing themselves as suffering and alienated, ignorant and jealous. In these two final examples from his sermon, Colegrove's negative terms are meant to get people excited about the possibility of change, to have them clap and yell in happy expectation of transforming their lives with God's power. First, he tells a gaudy version of the story in Mark 5:25–34 and Luke 8:43–48, in which a sick woman is miraculously healed by touching Jesus' clothes. In Mark, the woman is quoted as saying "If I may touch but his clothes, I shall be whole" (5:28). In his retelling, Colegrove exaggerates her character, giving her livelier words to speak: "Out of my way. I've gotta get to Jesus. Step aside. I've got to touch Jesus. For you see, I've got just enough faith, ha ha!—that if I can just touch him, I'm gonna leave here changed, I'm gonna leave here whole." This vivid example of persistence sets up Colegrove's claim, in the following excerpt, that "You just gotta get to Jesus":

> [Declaration:] You see, when you get desperate for an answer, when you get hungry for a change, you don't care what anybody thinks about you. You don't care what anybody says. You just gotta get to Jesus. [Promise:] People will talk about you. They always have, and they always will. But what does it matter, as long as I get to Jesus. Friends won't understand you, and they might make fun. But why would you care, as long as you can get to Jesus, I wisht somebody would get to Jesus right now. Do y'all hear me back there in the stands? [Action:] Lift up your voice to the Lord and somebody call on Him.

After this, Colegrove tells another Bible story, that of Bartimaeus from Mark 10:46–52. Bartimaeus, a blind man, is begging at the roadside when he hears that Jesus has come. He cries out for mercy from Jesus, and bystanders "charged him that he should hold his peace: but he cried the more a great deal, Thou Son of David, have mercy on me" (10:48). Again, Colegrove spikes the narrative with invented speech: "Friends told him, 'Bartimaeus, shut up! Quiet down. That's too much noise. We don't do that here.'" The preacher tells his audience, "before you leave to go to your home, Jesus is gonna walk your way," and pleads, "Please believe in me right now that God's gonna pour out His Spirit. Hallelujah. Hallelujah."

At this point, he confronts the gap between faith and knowledge:

[Declaration:] God is looking for those in this park tonight that can find enough faith that says, I don't understand the Holy Ghost, I don't really understand all there is to know about the Holy Ghost, and I can't explain speaking in tongues, and I really don't know why—yet—that I need the Holy Ghost. But you see what starts out small, when God gets in the picture, becomes greater. All you need tonight is just enough faith that says: [Promise:] I believe that the Holy Ghost can change my life. I believe that the Holy Ghost can release me from the bondage of sin. I believe that the Holy Ghost can set me loose from the powers of Hell. I may have come here to this park a drunk, but I'm gonna leave here set free. I may have come here tonight with hatred and with jealousy, but I'm leavin' here with the joy of the Lord in my soul. [Action:] Clap your hands to the Lord and praise Jesus. Hallelujah.

His statements about belief pivot smoothly between the categories of promise and action. "I believe that the Holy Ghost can release me from the bondage of sin" is not meant to sit in place like an inert proposition but to spur the listener to turn it into a promise for the future (you *will* be released from the bondage of sin) and to act upon it right now, bubbling up with noise like Bartimaeus.

The Altar Call

After his sermon, Colegrove calls on members of the audience to come to the space in front of the platform. He also urges faithful listeners to pull the reluctant along with them: "If you're standin' by somebody that needs the Holy Ghost, why don't you get 'em by the arm...." In the altar call, as in the sermon, Colegrove forges a looping path shaped by the pattern of declarations first, promises second, actions third.[2]

In the portion that I recorded—I was slightly late in switching on my recorder—he begins by alluding to Acts 2:38, saying, "Peter said the first thing you have to do is repent. Now I'm gonna ask everyone in this field tonight, if you already have the Holy Ghost or if you want the Holy Ghost, I want every one of us to repent." He exhorts people to repent of "every thought, every word, every deed" that is sinful, and explains, "after we have repented, then we're gonna begin to worship and praise the Lord." Then comes a remarkable stretch in which Colegrove teaches his listeners about glossolalia:

[Declaration:] People receive the Holy Ghost when they ask God for the Holy Ghost, and then begin to thank Him for it. [Promise:] Now when you receive the Holy Ghost, you're gonna speak in a language that you do not know. You're gonna say words that make no sense to you. There are gonna be words that come to your mind, you don't know what they are, but you say those words, speak those words out, because the Holy Ghost is making inter-cession for you. The Holy Ghost is praying through you, and God is going to fill every one of you with the Holy Ghost if you will do what I've been (asking) you.[3] The first thing is we're gonna repent. God will not come into a life that is full of sin. So we ask Him to forgive us. [Promise/Action:] And then I am gonna speak a word of faith, and when I command for you to receive the Holy Ghost, I want you to believe at that moment that God is gonna fill your mouth with the heavenly language, in the name of Jesus. [Action:] All right, let's everybody repent right now. Everybody repent of every word, every thought, every deed. "Jesus, I repent. I'm sorry, Lord. I want you to change my life. I want what Brother Colegrove has preached about tonight. I want the power of the Holy Ghost to come into my life. I'm sorry for all I have done against you, (God,) and I'm askin' you now to touch my life. Forgive me of my sins. I give my life to you, my purpose to serve you, God, in the name of Jesus." Hallelujah. C'mon, repent, ask God to forgive ya. I want the choir to sing. Hallelujah.

As in the sermon, during the altar call Colegrove tells his audience how to speak, coaching them into proper repentance. Never mind your lack of understanding, he is arguing, just do as I say, speak as I speak. In doing so, he is urging the audience to co-create a sense of unintelligibility which, although marked as unintelligible and not translated, is meant to yield a greater meaning (Tomlinson 2012a; see also Wirtz 2005, 2007).

To sustain the energy, he also tells the choir to begin singing. He does not stop at this point, but charges forth into a compact stretch of speech in which he issues commands, adds a few short declarations and promises, and concludes with direct commands and glossolalia of his own:

[Action:] Now if you repented of your sins, you've asked God to forgive ya, now I want you to begin to thank Him for forgiveness. Thank Him for forgiveness. [Promise:] Come on, the Holy Ghost is about to fall! [Action:] Begin to praise Him right now.

[Declaration:] He inhabits the praise of His people. (C'mon.) Your sins are under the blood, in the name of Jesus. [Promise:] Now when I speak the word of faith I want you to believe with me, [Action:] come on, right now. By the authority of the Word of God, I command you right now: receive ye the Holy Ghost! C'mon! *Sina-dyamaya-damai-pasata-nahaya!* [The choir begins to sing the repeated phrase, "Let it overflow."] My God, *anda-bakobasadaboha!* C'mon, that's right! Receive ye the Holy Ghost!...

Colegrove continues in this way, mixing glossolalia into his English exhortations while the choir sings. I am still in the grandstand and unable to hear the several dozen repenters who had gathered before the preaching platform, but, in retrospect, I take Colegrove's exclamation "C'mon, that's right!" as evidence that they are indeed speaking in tongues. I turn off my recorder after several minutes. Participants then go to a water tank near the grandstand to be baptized (Figure 2.2). I decide to leave at this point and take photographs from field level as I exit, dazzled but dazed.

So far, I have argued that Colegrove's speech is notable for its rhetorical movement from declaration to promise to action, following a looping

FIGURE 2.2 People being called for baptism during the Albert Park crusade.

path—a performative path, as I discuss later—which prompts his audience to move their bodies and to feel the Holy Ghost descending on Albert Park. The treatment I have offered so far is too thin, however, because if effective performance were simply a matter of speaking according to a well-crafted structure, it would be magic. Effectiveness does not lie in the words themselves but in the marriage of text and context framed by ideologies of how language works, how ritual works, and what counts as evidence of success or failure (Briggs 1988; Duranti and Goodwin 1992; Keane 1995, 1997, 2002, 2003, 2006, 2007; Sax 2010). What I have neglected so far is the wider context of performance expectations: what Pentecostal audiences expect to do when they show up at the door of the church, or the seats of the grandstand in Albert Park. "In the event of praising, we make noise," the Fijian Pentecostal pastor Ratu Meli Navuniyasi told the anthropologist Jacqueline Ryle. "Let everything that has breath make noise!...[T]he Word of God is not cold, it's hot—we call them spirit-filled preachers, filled with power, *mana*—God's *mana*" (Ryle 2001: 233). Believing that noise, heat, and power are effective elements of religious performance, Pentecostals are inclined to shout and jump around in a way that many other Christians are not. Such inclinations must be taught, and even though the majority of people in Albert Park probably already knew the lessons when they showed up that night, Colegrove took care to instruct people repeatedly on what to do and what to expect.[4]

Spinning in Stories

Colegrove's performance is deeply contoured by parallelism. As I have shown, he turns the pattern of declaration-promise-action into a continuous loop, following the same path again and again. He also repeats specific themes, words, and phrases within sections of his sermon. Here, I will show how the different levels of parallelism dovetail: specifically, how Colegrove's repetition of words and phrases helps mark his continual movement through the pattern of declaration-promise-action.

At the level of the entire sermon, Colegrove repeatedly expresses five main themes: (1) God is almighty; (2) God is here, or is going to come here, manifest as Jesus and the Holy Ghost; (3) God causes increase; (4) You are ignorant and sinful and need God's help; (5) You need to have faith and praise God now. He returns to these themes several times over the course of his sermon, giving his performance coherence through parallelism. Unlike Fijian Methodist preachers, who tend to lay things out point by point, Colegrove does not distinguish his themes neatly but runs them together in resonant repetition.

For example, he introduces the theme of God causing increase around one third of the way into his performance, declaring, "When God is a part of the equation, when God is a part of the composition, things that start out small get bigger." He refers to Jesus' parable of the mustard seed, a metaphor he will return to later (the mustard seed "is the least of all seeds: but when it is grown, it is the greatest among herbs, and becometh a tree," Matthew 13:32; see also Matthew 17:20, Mark 4:31, and Luke 13:19 and 17:6). Soon after this, when he tells the story of the sick woman as if it were a sporting event, he says: "The Bible says she pressed her way through the crowd. Men, big like these men, strong like these men, couldn't stand in her way. She pushed them aside like they were puppets." (By "these men," I believe he meant robust Fijians standing near him on the platform.) Swatting aside muscular men, she embodied the increased power of godliness. Later, in an excerpt already quoted, Colegrove tells the audience that their ignorance of the Holy Ghost does not matter—"God is looking for those in this park tonight that can find enough faith that says, I don't understand the Holy Ghost"—and he goes on to explain, "you see what starts out small, when God gets in the picture, becomes greater." He also urges the audience to "magnify" Jesus by clapping.

These themes are occasionally elaborated through another parallel structure in which Colegrove shifts from speaking in a biblical register to a folksy Texas one. For example, recall the moment described when he quotes the verses 1 Peter 1:4–5 on the subject of faith and salvation ("To an inheritance incorruptible and undefiled..."), and then goes on to explain, "I'm preachin' about faith that brings salvation, faith that's gonna take you somewhere." Another example comes when he preaches, "Jesus declared in John chapter seven, 'he that believeth on me'—who's gonna believe on Jesus tonight?—as the Scripture has said, 'out of his belly shall flow rivers of living water. (This he spake of the Holy Ghost which they that believe on Him should receive.)'" In this short stretch Colegrove quotes the Bible, but interrupts with a question that grafts the King James Version's archaic "believe on" with his own down-home "who's gonna." He follows this by announcing, "Ladies and gentlemen, it is God's will, it is His divine purpose, that you leave this place tonight filled with the baptism of the Holy Ghost," a statement phrased formally but not quite biblically. Finally, he concludes with an informal statement that is pure Texan: "It's time to kick the Devil out and welcome Jesus in." The alternating registers in Colegrove's sermon resonate with each other and suggest that the lessons of the Bible are directly applicable to people's experiences today.

Colegrove's most obvious parallelism is his word-by-word repetition. This includes simple structures ("Hallelujah. Hallelujah") and complex ones ("If

you've got your hope in money, that's a dead hope. If you've got your hope
in friends, that's a dead hope. If you've got your...hope in what government
might do, that's a dead hope"). The key terms "believe," "faith," and "feel"
cluster in dense pockets: for example, in one stretch of thirty-four words he
says "believe" five times; in one stretch of sixty-six words he says "faith" ten
times; and in one stretch of sixty-two words he says "feel" seven times. In
addition, Colegrove sometimes chains his repetitions together, which can
generate a sense of expectation as well as completion. That is, when he
preaches "I believe that the Holy Ghost can change my life. I believe that the
Holy Ghost can release me from the bondage of sin," listeners who are participating imaginatively can almost begin preaching themselves, beginning
with "I believe that the Holy Ghost can..." and finishing with a general statement of belief. If they do, they will echo Colegrove, who concludes, "I believe
that the Holy Ghost can set me loose from the powers of Hell." Parallelism,
in sum, can create a sense of familiarity through repetition and also a sense
of prospective momentum, an expectation that things will be completed in a
definite way that helps to reveal what people already know.[5]

Transcribed on the page, this chained parallelism creates an image of
cascading text. When the words of a preacher like Colegrove are written
down, point and line guide the reader's eyes across the canvas of the page.
Consider the part of his sermon in which he says:

> The Bible tells us in Hebrews chapter eleven that without faith it is
> impossible to please Him, for he that cometh to the Lord—whoo!
> hallelujah—must believe that He is. I believe I'm preaching tonight
> to people tonight who believe that He is. That He is Jesus, He is
> almighty, He is the alpha and the omega, the beginning and the
> end, the first and the last, which was, which is, and is to come, the
> almighty God. I believe I'm preachin' to people today that believe
> that He is our only hope. He is our deliverance from sin.

Beginning at the end of the second sentence, "who believe that He is,"
Colegrove shapes his phrases in dense and detailed parallelism, as shown
in Text 2.1. Repeated words are lined up in columns and boldfaced. Laid out
like this, the word-by-word and phrase-by-phrase structure of Colegrove's
poetry is impressive. He is spinning out stories and also spinning in
stories, building resonance by echoing himself and gaining rhetorical
momentum through repetition.

But this kind of parallelism, in and of itself, reveals little. A clumsy orator can use parallelism perfectly by saying the same things over and over

Text 2.1

... believe that He is

I believe I'm preaching tonight to people tonight who
believe that He is.
That He is Jesus,
He is almighty,
He is the alpha and the omega,
the beginning and the end,
the first and the last, which was,
which is,
and is to come, the almighty God.

I believe I'm preachin' to people today that
believe that He is our only hope.
He is our deliverance
from sin.

Text 2.2

[Declaration:]

The stage has been set.
The atmosphere has been charged. Faith is in this place.

[Promise:]

And I believe—I wisht I could find someone else who will
believe—
I believe that God is going to do miracles here tonight.
I believe God is going to heal sick bodies tonight.
I believe that God is going to fill people.. .

[Action:]
Praise God, *haya-boko-taya-bahaya*, whoo!
Praise God.
Praise God, come on, clap your hands to the Lord again.

---

again. Colegrove, however, is a verbal acrobat, and his microparallelism—his repetition of words and phrases—often dovetails with the pattern of declaration-promise-action, as seen in the moment when he first speaks in tongues (Text 2.2).

The declaration segment is a self-contained unit of statements stitched together by the repetition of "The...has been, The...has been." The promise segment is also a self-contained unit, with statements of belief joined in parallel units of "I believe, I believe (that)" and "God is going to...tonight." Finally, the action segment features commands, glossolalia, and a whoop, grouped together in the units of "Praise God, Praise God." Not every section of Colegrove's sermon displays perfect alignment like this, but the complexities and imperfections do not fundamentally disturb the larger pattern.

Performative Paths

The sermon and altar call consistently follow the pattern of declaration-promise-action. But Colegrove is not singing a one-note song: he is a flexible performer, adapting Bible stories with flair, making brief comments on the context of performance, and explaining his doctrine to a new audience, mostly to indicate that people shouldn't actually think about it too much. In other words, he does many things in his performance, all woven together in the three-part pattern. But why should he use this method? And what effect does it have?

The answers must be understood in terms of the metaphorical motion of entextualization. As discussed in Chapter 1, I am calling the kind of motion seen in Colegrove's sermon and altar call *performative paths*, or patterned sequences meant to generate ritual efficacy. The movement between declarations, promises, and actions is not physical movement but the continual articulation of a rhetorical pattern. Colegrove repeatedly connects statements about what the world is like with statements about what should happen, and connects statements about what should happen with commands to make it happen now, as well as thanksgiving to God for having it happen this way. In moving along this path, Colegrove repeatedly leads people from thought to hope to deed. His rhetorical patterns reflect the classic Christian model of three stages of humanity's progress: "*before Christ*, when men lived in sin, *from Christ to Judgment*, when men lived in hope of redemption, and *kingdom come*," which, as Sahlins observes, is itself a theological version of the unlineal evolutionary sequence of savagery, barbarism, and civilization (1996: 400–401 n. 18; emphasis in original). Colegrove characterizes his audience as sinful, then offers hope of change, and then attempts to get audience members to connect with God by praising him, and, in a climactic moment, speaking *as* God by speaking in tongues. In this way, an eternity of human relationship to the divine, in Christian understandings, is condensed, reflected, and remade in the performance.

As a performer, Colegrove operates on two levels. First, moment by moment, he commands his audience and utters performative statements like "praise God" and "thank you, Jesus," which are themselves acts of praising and thanking. (Their functional equivalent is "Hallelujah," from the Hebrew for "Praise Jehovah," which Colegrove says more than twenty times during the sermon and altar call.) His glossolalia, too, is performative. Although it does not have a literal meaning for English-, Fijian-, or Fiji Hindi-speaking audience members, a phrase such as *anda-bakobasadaboha* carries performative force because it accomplishes what Colegrove has been talking about all along: the Holy Ghost is here, now, manifest in speech. It is a kind of performativity that is devoid of semantic meaning, though evidently considered deeply meaningful. The radical otherness of the language reflects God's ultimate otherness (Tomlinson 2012a; see also Bialecki 2011; Stasch 2012). Second, as a total event, the crusade must be seen as performativity writ large, because the preacher is attempting to compel not only his listeners but also to compel God to act for everyone in response to the entire performance. His words, and his audience's physical responses, are meant to make divine action happen. Textual motion prompts physical motion which prompts divine motion, with the Holy Ghost about to fall and Jesus ready to walk through Albert Park. Colegrove says at one point (quoted earlier), "let's let God do somethin' here tonight," suggesting that although God is the supreme actor, it is humanity's task to create a ritual context conducive to God's action. Later, about halfway through his sermon, he preaches: "I didn't have to worry tonight whether or not Jesus was gonna be here, because as soon as I stepped into the park and heard the praises of this choir, and heard the sounds of magnification and rejoicing to the Lord, it let me know that God was gonna be here." Feel the wounds of sin deeply enough, and shout loud enough, Colegrove is saying, and God must respond.[6]

Other Christian preachers can use different patterns of entextualization, obviously. Not everyone preaches according to the declaration-promise-action plan. To show why this matters, I briefly consider part of a sermon delivered by a Fijian Methodist catechist and then compare both Pentecostalism and Methodism with traditional indigenous Fijian oratory.

Methodist preaching can resemble Colegrove's firestorm in some ways—for example, some Methodist preachers are poetic composers who use parallelism artfully, and some yell with sustained intensity—but the differences are stark. Methodist services are highly formal, and speakers do not usually receive much response from their seated congregations beyond an occasional "good, thanks" (*vinaka*). No one speaks in tongues. Most significantly, preachers give few commands to their congregations, and when they do, the commands do not usually compel immediate physical action but pertain to general matters of conduct (for example, "Let us not depend a lot on worldly things" or "Do not build yourself up").

The sermon excerpt I analyze was delivered by the Methodist catechist Tomasi Laveasiga in the Tavuki village church on Pentecost Sunday, May 23, 1999.[7] In this section, he explains the meaning of Pentecost and the nature of the Holy Spirit (Text 2.3).

Although this sermon deals with the same general topic as Colegrove's— the inspiration of the Holy Ghost/Holy Spirit—the styles of presentation are entirely different. Colegrove acknowledges that his listeners might be ignorant about the Holy Ghost's divine nature, but he tries to push people past their hesitations to act immediately despite their lack of knowledge. Laveasiga, by contrast, takes pains to explain what the Holy Spirit is. He moves methodically with a biblical compass: the prophet Joel foretold Pentecost, which is described in Acts; the Holy Spirit can be traced to the account of creation in the book of Genesis. He offers three glosses to help his audience conceptualize the Holy Spirit: it is God's spirit, it is wind, it is breath. Later, he adds that there are two paths by which the Holy Spirit comes into the world, "the whistling wind...[and] the flame" (*na cagi vace-varuru...na yameyame ni buka*).

Another notable difference between the performances is that Colegrove wants people to be excited by the newness that the Holy Ghost offers them, whereas Laveasiga wants people to appreciate the old, time-tested basis of what he is saying. Although Colegrove does not use the words "old" or "new," his message sets up a parallel between sinfulness and the past—the recent past of people's lives, not the remote and idealized past of the Bible—counterposed to blessedness and the future. His characterization of audience members is generally negative, painting an unflattering portrait of how they have lived their lives so far: "What you need is not another drug addiction," he preaches at one point, "What you need is not another hang-up. What you need is not another problem. You don't need your alcoholism." In contrast to this, he promises something novel and

Text 2.3

Na Sigatabu nidavu...i dua na siga na siga nidavu, vananuma jiko ke na siga ni Penitiko, i dua na siga sa yalatakina tu o Joeli na parofita ni vo jiko i vica na drau na yabaki me sucu ko Jisu.

Noda lesoni da rogoca na jikina e jinikavitu: "A sa kaya na Kalou ena yaco ena gauna maimuri sovaraka kina na yaloqu vei ira na tamata kecega." Ka na itukutuku tukuna ko Joeli qai mai vavoutakina o Luke ni vola na ikarua ni nona ivola ka vakatokai nodra cakacaka na iapositolo. I mino walega ni qai je ere vou i na Ivola Tabu na Yalo Tabu. Je sovaraki na Yalo Tabu, je na Yalo Tabu ka mai lajiva i noda lesoni ina bogibogi nidavu. I mini je ere vou na itukutuku ni Vola Tabu raraba. Na Yalo Tabu na yalo ni Kalou.

Na Ivakajekivu wase e dua: ni jekivu me buli na vuravura, se bera ni dua na ere i buli i vuravura. Tukuna jiko vei keda na Ivakajekivu kevani da na wilika, "A sa yavavala na yalo ni Kalou ena dela ni wai." Na yalo ni Kalou na Yalo Tabu. I mini je ere vou i na itukutuku ni Vola Tabu na Yalo Tabu. Se bera ni buli i dua na ere buli i vuravura, ina vuravura ni veibuli ka da bula ke, ma sa jiko rawa na Yalo Tabu.

I na Ivola Tabu vou, je na Ivola Tabu, na Yalo Tabu, kena ibalebale i rua na ere. Na imatai na cagi. Kena...ikarua na icegu. Na ibalebale ni Yalo Tabu i na Ivola Tabu na cagi vata kei na cegu.

This Sunday...is a day commemorating the day of Pentecost, a day the prophet Joel promised a few hundred years before Jesus was born.

[For] our Bible reading we heard [Acts 2] verse seventeen: "And it shall come to pass in the last days, saith God, I will pour out of my Spirit upon all flesh." This is the story Joel told, and Luke retold when he wrote his second book which is called the Acts of the Apostles. The Holy Spirit is not something new in the Bible. The Holy Spirit was poured forth, it was the Holy Spirit that was seen in our Bible reading this morning. The whole Bible is not something new. The Holy Spirit is God's spirit.

Genesis chapter one: when the world was beginning to be created, when nothing was created yet in the world. Genesis tells us if we will read it, "And the Spirit of God moved upon the face of the waters." God's spirit is the Holy Spirit. In the Bible's stories, the Holy Spirit is not something new. Before anything was created in the world, in the world of creation where we live, the Holy Spirit existed.

In the New Testament, or the Bible, the Holy Spirit means two things. The first is wind. The...second is breath. The meaning of Holy Spirit in the Bible is wind and breath.

---

transformative: "Faith that's going to turn your life upside down, faith that's going to destroy the power of sin in your life, faith that's going to give you deliverance through the name of Jesus." Laveasiga, in exemplary Fijian Methodist fashion, grounds his claims by saying that he is not offering anything new at all, implying that what he presents is old and therefore reliable. In the excerpt he makes this point three times, emphasizing that the Bible and its stories about the Holy Spirit are not anything new (*i mini je ere vou*). I believe Laveasiga repeated these points as a way of reassuring his audience, who might be wary of too intense a focus on the Holy Spirit and glossolalia—these being favored subjects of groups like Pentecostals, who have pared members away from the Methodist Church in recent years.

A third difference, the treatment of individual versus collective subjects, illuminates the larger purpose that each performance is meant to achieve. Colegrove focuses relentlessly on individuals. His goal is to save individual souls against the resistance of an unbelieving public. He describes friends as obstacles: "Friends won't understand you, and they might make fun." More generally, "People will talk about you. They always have, and they always will." Laveasiga's subject is indigenous Fijian society, not the individuals who comprise it. He says, in parts of his sermon not quoted here, that the Holy Spirit both causes and indicates unity: it causes groups to be united and comes to groups that are united. The trigger for his sermon was the recent national election, whose results deeply upset many people in Tavuki and eventually led to the coup of 2000. To some extent, Colegrove would presumably agree with the Methodist sermon: he wants everyone acting in unison, too. But Colegrove wants people acting together in specifically physical ways, here and now, to achieve their individual salvation, whereas Laveasiga focuses on the way unity serves the *vanua*, the indigenous Fijian body politic organized under chiefs (Tomlinson 2009: 177–182).

But the most striking difference between the two performances is their configuration as performative paths. Colegrove's is a path within itself; Laveasiga's is not. Laveasiga, unlike Colegrove, sticks to declarations. He adds a few promises, but he does not command. Sentence after sentence, declarative statements roll in like waves. This is true of his entire sermon. (The only statement in the quoted excerpt that is not a declaration is God's promise, "And it shall come to pass in the last days, saith God, I will pour out of my Spirit upon all flesh," but even this is embedded in the declarative phrase "we heard verse seventeen..."). Although different Methodist preachers develop distinct styles, with differing degrees of verbal artistry, Laveasiga's approach is broadly representative. Methodist sermons do not move from declaration to promise to action, but stick mostly to declaration. Topics are often numbered by preachers, so their sermons follow a sequence in this way, but the kinds of statements that Methodist preachers unfurl under each topic all resemble each other and do not develop a complex pattern within and among themselves. The performative path that makes Methodist sermons effective ritual actions is the sequence of the whole church service in which sermons follow prayers, hymns, speeches, and money collection, and come near the end of the event as general statements of truth and exhortation. That is, Methodist sermons are meant to accurately represent God's relationship to humanity and to encourage people to live up to divine models in their daily lives. These statements and exhortations mark an effective worship service by being articulated with the larger structure, within which the sermon is the main event. Colegrove's performance, in comparison, is a self-contained performative path. Again and again, he loops from declaration to promise to action and back again, generating a sense of expectation and then, when his commands receive a response, a sense of completion as well.[8] His sermon and altar call also gain efficacy by being embedded within the larger context of the crusade, but textually speaking, Colegrove's speech follows a clear and distinct performative path of its own in a way that Methodist sermons such as Laveasiga's do not.

Within indigenous Fijian traditional oratory, however, there is a type of speech that follows the declaration-promise-action pattern seen in Colegrove's performance. This is formal speeches of acceptance, such as the acceptance of kava presented ceremonially between guests and hosts (*[i]sevusevu*). A good example of such a text is given by Andrew Arno (1985: 131). He asked villagers for model speeches, and the one in Text 2.4 was given "as a simulated acceptance speech on behalf of a chief who has been asked permission to visit the island by an American scholar." The first half of this speech is a series of declarations, describing the situation that is unfolding: "I accept the kava of chiefs.... The gentleman from America...comes here to learn about our islands." The speaker then switches to statements that are future-oriented. He lists a series of hoped-for situations that will result from the exchange of kava: kinship will be solidified, customs honored, the church prosperous, the land bountiful, the people blessed, and the research successful. These statements are phrased as declarations in the Fijian version, but their fulfillment is tied

Text 2.4

Au tara saka mada ga na yaqona vakaturaga.	Sir, I accept the kava of chiefs.
Cabe vakaturaga tu mai na Sevusevu.	It comes up in the noble way, this Sevusevu.
Cabe vakaturaga tu mai vua na Turaga ni Merikei.	It comes up in the noble way from The gentleman from America.
Ka laki tu mai vakavuli	Who comes here to learn
Ki na noda veiyanuyanu.	about our islands.
Lako tu mai ki na vanua....	He comes here to the land...
Sevusevu tu ni bula.	Sevusevu of life.
[*Response*: Vinaka, Vinaka.]	[Good, Good.]
Sevusevu tu ni dei.	Sevusevu for the *vanua* to stand firm.
Dei tu ai sala vakaveiwekani	May the way of kinship be firmly fixed.
Dei tu ai tovo vakavanua.	May the customs of the land be firmly fixed.
[*Response*: Vinaka, Saka.]	[Good, Sir.]
Taura va'vaqara tiko lomalagi	I accept this and offer it up to heaven
Sobu tu a kena veivakalougatataki.	So that its blessings descend.
Tubu a lotu.	May religion grow strong.
Sautu e dela ni vanua.	May the land be bountiful.
Tau na lagi, ruru tu ni cagi e na yabaki.	Let the rain fall and the winds be gentle throughout the year.
Cabe tu na ika mai takali.	Let fish rise up from the open sea.
Taura va'vaqara tiko lomalagi	I take this and offer it up to heaven.
Sobu mai kena veivakalougatataki.	May its blessings descend.
Loma dua na Kalou.	That we may be in accord with God.
Ka rawata mada ga na i lakolako vakavuli!	And may the scholarly journey be accomplished!

to the ceremony's success and projected into the future (see also Tuwere 2002: 63). The promises are interrupted only when the speaker says twice that he is accepting the kava to "offer it up to heaven." After the promise section comes the line in which the speech gains its performative force, accomplishing what has been described: "Mana, e dina, a muduo."[9] *Mana* is a verb denoting effecting action; *e dina* means "it is true"; *a muduo* is a men's expression used in thanks for things like food and valuables (Paul Geraghty, personal communication, June 29, 2010; see also Hocart

1929: 71 n. 12; Tabana ni Vosa kei Na iTovo Vakaviti 2005: 6). When uttered at the end of a ritual such as a *sevusevu*, the phrase "terminates a unit of liturgy like the Christian 'Amen'" (Tuwere 2002: 137) and makes the preceding words effective.

Formal speeches of acceptance, like the one described by Arno, thus follow the declaration-promise-action pattern. They are much briefer than Colegrove's performance and feature more strictly formulaic speech, but they follow the same performative path. A striking irony, then, is that Colegrove's speech resembles traditional Fijian oratory in this way whereas Methodist sermons do not, even though the latter carry an aura of "traditionality" that Pentecostal performances utterly lack in Fiji. In other words, Pentecostalism is seen by many Fijian Methodists as being completely out of step with traditional Fijian cultural values, but in terms of entextualization, a Pentecostal sermon like Colegrove's resembles traditional Fijian oratory more than a Methodist sermon like Laveasiga's does. However, other genres of Methodist performance may follow the declaration-promise-action pattern; for example, one extended prayer of exorcism that I have examined in previous publications does this (Tomlinson 2004: 12; 2009: 151–153; see Tomlinson 2002: 316–318 for the complete text).

For performative paths, other patterns exist besides the declaration-promise-action pattern I have examined in this chapter. In Chapter 1, I discussed Joel Kuipers's example of Weyewa ceremonies held to restore good relations with the ancestors. Over the course of these ceremonies, mediums progressively use fewer and fewer examples of direct reported speech from the spirits, creating an impression of many individual agents cohering into unity. Another example comes from Godfrey Lienhardt's classic discussion of theology and ritual among the Dinka people of Sudan. Examining the language of sacrificial rites, he writes:

> Everything which the Dinka desire is stated many times and these repetitions themselves are chorused by the rest of the company. This rhythmical repetition of particular sets of words and ideas, spoken first singly then in unison, gradually has an effect which may be observed by anyone attending a sacrifice and, moreover, comes to be felt by the foreign observer himself. At the beginning of such a ceremony there is usually a lot of chatter and disorder.

People come and go, greet each other, discuss their private affairs, change their places, and so on... .

As the invocations increase in tempo, however, the little bursts of incisive speech by the invoker and his chorus draw the congregation more and more towards the central action. In theory (though not always in practice) the senior and most important men speak their invocations last, when the others have prepared the congregation for them. As the invocations proceed, the repeaters of the invocations work together more smoothly in rhythmical speech, and a collective concentration upon the main theme and purpose of the gathering becomes apparent.

This concentration of attention on a single action ends when the sacrificial victim is thrown and killed, and there is then a sensible release of a tension which has been slowly mounting throughout the ceremony.... It is thus at the moment immediately preceding the physical death of the beast, as the last invocation reaches its climax with more vigorous thrusts of the spear, that those attending the ceremony are most palpably members of a single undifferentiated body, looking towards a single common end. (Lienhardt 1961: 233)

Like Kuipers's example of Weyewa ritual speech, the Dinka ceremony described by Lienhardt follows a performative path of unification: from chatter to chant, from many voices to one. In the Dinka sacrifice, which Lienhardt presents in none-too-subtle sexual tones, collective invocations grow quicker, smoother, and more rhythmical as people grow "palpably" unified in approaching their final collective action, the killing of cattle.

Other striking examples of performative paths can be found in the literature on séances and shamanism from Papua New Guinea and Indonesia. Feld (1982) and Schieffelin (1985) describe Kaluli performers who heighten audience tension in specific, structured ways as they sing in the voices of deceased ancestors, revealing the landscape that spirits "see" until the deceased's intimate relations recognize the spirits' identities and burst into tears. Atkinson (1989) observes how Wana shamans attempt to engage their audiences by having their spirit familiars request particular food or objects. The spirits speak poetically and metaphorically, and audiences are supposed to guess what they really want. In some cases, shamans become frustrated when the audience—bored, sleepy, distracted—ignores their spirits' requests; such ritual failure is considered potentially dangerous both for the shaman and the community. In other cases, however, spirit and audience engage in dialogues in which the latter solves the riddling language, giving the spirits what they seek if it is available and thereby ensuring a successful performance, which enhances the shaman's reputation. In these examples, performers speak in patterned ways that help generate audiences' senses that a transformation is taking place: new information is gained, spirits are appeased, and sick people are healed.

In many ways, the crusade held by the United Pentecostal Church International of Fiji on December 4, 2008, was a small and fleeting event. The visiting preacher was not a global superstar like Billy Graham or Benny Hinn. It was just one night in the course of a weeklong program, and the crowd fit easily into one corner of a small city park. In this chapter I have argued that the event deserves close scholarly attention, however, for the way it reveals a distinct pattern of entextualization and its ritual effects. In performative paths, different parts articulate with each other in sequence; ritual performances gain their perceived effectiveness from the links between the different parts, and the larger pattern encourages the construction of distinct kinds of selves. Kenneth Colegrove's sermon and altar call cycled continually from declaration to promise to action as it moved among several overlapping parallel structures. The preacher followed a performative path in which rhetorical movement was designed to provoke physical movement—to make people clap and shout with urgency, with exuberant joy in order to make themselves ecstatic Christians whose salvation would be seen and heard when God spoke through them.[10]

3

Crossed Signs

EARLY IN 2009, I began a new research project by tabulating the bachelors' and masters' theses at the Pacific Theological College (PTC) in Suva. The college is international and ecumenical, so it has students from all parts of the Pacific studying a wide range of topics. As I worked my way through the collection, noting authors, titles, and subjects, I found myself caught up in reading some of the theses in detail, either because their titles were captivating or because I knew, or wanted to know, something about their authors' identities. Several of the authors have become highly influential in the region, such as Winston Halapua (B.D., 1971), who is now one of three archbishops in the Anglican Church of Aotearoa, New Zealand and Polynesia. One had become notorious: Djoubelly Wea (B.D., 1977) assassinated the New Caledonian independence leader Jean-Marie Tjibaou and was immediately killed himself. I was especially intrigued to find that a number of the Fijian Methodist Church's top leaders had received degrees from PTC. Considering Fijian Methodism's conservatism and PTC's progressivism, this was a surprisingly fruitful match.

As I began reading theses, I became riveted by discussions of the beverage kava, which is consumed frequently and enthusiastically by many of Fiji's citizens and is an icon of indigenous tradition. Several of the Fijian students pointed out a parallel between kava-drinking sessions and Christian communion which had been running through my own thinking. To illustrate, I will quote at length from a bachelor's thesis written in 1973 by Jovili Meo, who would later become PTC's principal:

> Our present orders of the Lord's Supper have very little response from the people. I think it is time that we should structure a more

Fijian order which is more meaningful to us, and this means the renewal of the whole structure. Because Jesus used this very simple and common thing, the family meal setting for his memory. We also likewise can use common everyday life meetings, for example, kava drinking, feasting and "baptise" them for christian usage....

An indigenised order should be set inside a Fijian bure (a meeting house or the local church) where the villagers normally meet. The people are seated cross-legged as if they are ready for kava drinking. At one point of the circle sits the chief and others sit around him. Opposite the chief is the minister with the elements. The seating itself illustrates the nature of the minister, namely he is a servant. He does not stand from "up there" facing the people, but he sits with them....

Indigenous worship means the use of locally-made wooden plates or baskets (made from coconut leaves) for the bread and a "tanoa" [kava bowl] for the wine, which is to be served in small cups made of coconut shells. The recipients of the elements may clap their hands as a sign of acceptance and thanksgiving. The whole kava ceremony itself, if used for the Lord's Supper brings with [it] strong feelings of brotherhood and generosity.

I have experimented with this method twice with Fijian critics participating and the majority of them including faculty members and students of the Pacific Theological College commented that they had not been very close to each other until that experience. I hope that more performances will encourage Fijians to see the usefulness of our customs which can be used for the glory of God and also that they can experience something meaningful in their lives. (Meo 1973: 132–134)

There are three noteworthy things about this passage. The first is that despite Meo's reasonable argument, and the fact that participants reportedly said they felt closer to each other when communion was conducted in the style of a kava session, this model has not been adopted. Specifically, I have never seen or heard of any other contemporary Fijian Methodists serving communion wine as if it were kava, in coconut shells from a kava bowl, or seating themselves at communion as if they were at a kava-drinking session. Second, Meo uses the term "critics" for his audience, as if anticipating a negative reaction—or perhaps he had already been told that his experiment would fail. Third, and most remarkably, despite its ingenuity and boldness the experiment goes only halfway. If one really wants to give communion a "more Fijian order," which will therefore be "more meaningful," why not actually replace wine with kava?

It might seem that the ritual of holy communion offers Fijian Methodists an ideal opportunity to unite their most cherished public identities: they are good Christians who honor their *vanua* (land and people, connoting the traditional order under chiefly authority). Using kava for wine—and, say, taro for bread—would seem to join these symbols effectively. Roman Catholics in Pohnpei, Micronesia, use kava to conduct a reconciliation ritual that formally resembles communion in several respects: it takes place in church, a kava plant is placed on the altar, part of it is cut off and then pounded in preparation for drinking, and the priest, receiving the first cup, "turns toward the altar with the cup in his hand, prays to God for forgiveness for himself and for the community, then drinks the cup in God's name to show that God does extend his forgiveness to the community" (McGrath 1973: 66).[1] And there are examples of indigenous substances other than kava being used in communion. At a PTC chapel service in February 2009, the Maohi (French Polynesian) service leader mentioned that a well-known leader of the Free Wesleyan Church of Tonga had visited Tahiti in 1986 and given communion there with breadfruit and coconut juice instead of bread and wine. Further afield, James Fox (2011) describes how Rotenese members of the Protestant Evangelical Church of Timor dye local gin red for use in communion.[2]

There are, however, deeply rooted reasons to explain why Fijian Methodists do not make this kind of substitution, as I explain in this chapter. I suspect Meo knew that an experiment in which kava was used as the symbol of Christ's blood would cause considerable offense. Nonetheless, the logical force is compelling, especially when one considers how kava ceremonies and communion follow the same pattern of entextualization, *chiasmus*. Chiasmus is an X-shaped pattern of "criss-cross reciprocation" (Silverstein 2004: 626). When seen in terms of their ritual textuality, Christian communion and Fijian kava sessions look remarkably similar: in both, people who consume a sacred substance incorporate its associated social order into themselves while incorporating themselves into this social order.

Chiasmus

The example of holy communion shows how chiasmus involves two simultaneous movements that are figuratively X-shaped in relation to each other. In eating consecrated bread and drinking consecrated wine,

Methodists (and all Protestants) symbolically take Christ into themselves and put themselves into Christ, a metaphor of the Christian church.[3] In short, communicants incorporate Christ's body into theirs while incorporating themselves into the body of Christ. In this compact way, Christ the person is brought into conjunction with Christ the institution (the church and its members), and the resonant themes of past and present, humanity and divinity, and immanence and transcendence are all united through "crossing" each other in ritual.

Michael Silverstein characterizes ritual in general—not only chiasmus—in terms of motion: "Ritual as enacted traces a moving structure of indexical gestures toward the knowledge presupposed to be necessary to its own effectiveness in accomplishing something" (2004: 626). That is, as ritual unfolds over time, its semiotic configurations shift, continually pointing toward the underlying expectations of how the formal action does what it does. Participants' actions articulate with larger structures of action and participation, and "it is the overall 'poetry' as well as the particular forms of such manipulation of signs that count toward performing a ritual correctly" (626). He is worth quoting at length for his intricate analysis of motion, poetics, and experience:

> Ritual can be verbal or nonverbal or, as is usually the case, a combination of multiple modalities of figuration played out in an orderly—the technical term, as in poetry, is "metricalized"—space-time envelope of participation. The very hypertrophic orderliness of multiple metricalizations thus bounds the performed text of ritual, giving it a semblance of formal plenitude-in-itself. In and by this property of seeming to self-entextualize, to stand as [a] formally autonomous totality, a ritual text as a whole traced over space-time projects as its contextualization that which it dynamically figurates along a "cosmic axis," an axis of knowledge or belief. Such dynamic, directional spatiotemporal movements in ritual entail in this fashion the causal (re)ordering of cosmic conceptualizations as figurally indexed, such as aspects of sacred or foundational knowledge, feeling, and belief, made figurally "real" in the here-and-now of experienceable semiosis. (Silverstein 2004: 626; see also Silverstein 1992)

Silverstein is observing how ritual texts, in their orderly articulation, can give a convincing completeness to action as they both create and point to the context for that action's effectiveness. This was seen in the sermon and altar call of Pentecostal preacher Kenneth Colegrove, analyzed in Chapter 2: all of his verbal and physical dynamism was geared toward generating a sense of eternal truths which his audience already "knew." He amplified this humming self-knowledge with the crackle of instant opportunity: God's salvation is always available to you, but you need to seize this moment right now.

Chiasmus "seem[s] to self-entextualize," as Silverstein puts it, by the logic of conjunction. It unites counterposed elements in an X-shaped pattern whose formal effect is to both enact and transcend metaphor. The reciprocation involves a modal shift that is crucial to fostering people's senses of ritual effectiveness. The first action is a physical one: a congregant eats a wafer and drinks wine. The second action is an act of imaginative participation: one affirms one's membership in the church, or, to switch the roles of agent and patient, the church incorporates the congregant. The accomplishment of the first is manifest in the moment of action itself (consumption); the accomplishment of the second is manifest later, in the discourse that takes the action (participation) as presupposed. The first action prefigures the success of the second one, and the second fulfills the first. Neither part works without the other, but the two "lines" in the X-shaped relationship are distinct.[4]

The formal properties of chiasmus can give it a dangerous aspect as an inherently effective ritual form which can be tragically skewed or deviously reordered. For example, Douglas Lewis (n.d.) describes an incident in Flores, Indonesia, in which a man who was invoking a god by chanting in parallel couplets mistakenly said "Mother land and earth above, Father sun and moon below," rather than the correct "Mother land and earth below, Father sun and moon above." This was considered a major error because by transposing "above" and "below," the chanter figuratively turned the world upside down. The night he made this error, he died. Lewis observes that he "died from a chiasmus, a verbal catastrophe by which he inverted the order of the world."

Another example of chiasmus's dangerous aspect comes from Vicente Rafael's analysis of blood oaths in the Philippines. Centuries ago, the explorer Magellan and the Philippines' first governor-general had "both entered into blood compacts with local chiefs as a way to establish alliances with them" (Rafael 2009: 229). In the nineteenth century, Filipino nationalists represented these founding events in terms of friendship and equality, and a promise of fruitful combination that would eventually turn Filipinos into Spaniards. But the nationalists saw their own age negatively: the Spaniards' promises had not been upheld, a single gene-alogy had not been formed, and "centuries of Spanish abuse amounted to a betrayal of this ancient agreement" (2009: 230). Filipinos were thus no longer obligated to honor the original compact. Instead, they created a new one, secret blood oaths in which an initiate's arm was cut and he signed a pledge with his blood.

The earlier blood compact—the idealized one of Magellan and the local chiefs—had ritually echoed communion, but the Spanish had not seen it as a threat because it was conducted on their own terms. In contrast, the nationalist appropriation was seen as a devilish perversion: "By entering into a blood compact," Rafael writes of Spanish perceptions, "Filipinos become possessed. The oath turns them into monstrous figures" (2009: 231). The colonists were horrified, and wild rumors dashed off in every direction. The source of their horror was the chiasmus that defines Christian com-munion—or, rather, the fact that Filipinos were recognizably repeating the pattern in which blood and sacrifice are conjoined, but doing so for new and exclusive purposes. The initiates were giving their blood to the cause of independence and in doing so were being asked to take the blood of Spaniards if necessary. The colonists reacted with maddened revulsion at the rumors, repulsed and mortified at the way chiasmus' orderliness had made communion available for demonic subversion.[5]

In some rituals, chiasmus does not elicit such stark moral evaluations; rather, it articulates the power of the past with the transformed present in a morally ambiguous way. For example, Geoffrey White describes a legend of Santa Isabel, Solomon Islands, in which the first paramount chief to convert to Christianity cut off the head of a child "and with his warriors drank the blood of the Child to mark his conversion to Christianity, and renounce his allegiance to his god" (White 2013: 189). In Santa Isabel, where people have long been passionately engaged in projects of reconcil-ing Anglican authority with chiefly authority, this story is well known and retold at chiefly installations because it so vividly marks off the violence of the past from the present pax Christiana—but it does so not by separating those elements, but by joining them. The story, presented dramatically and "repeated verbatim over the course of decades," according to White, "work[s] to (re)situate the idea of paramount chief at a prominent juncture between *kastom* [custom, tradition] and Christianity" (White 2013: 190; see also White 1991: 225). As I now argue, indigenous Fijian kava-drinking sessions similarly unite counterposed elements in a reconciliation focused on the power of chiefs in the present.

Still Land, Moving People

Indigenous Fijian kava-drinking sessions can be seen as acts of communion because their pattern of chiasmus creates a social order. As in holy communion, in kava sessions people take an indexical sign (the kava itself) of the social order into themselves as they thereby create that social order and situate themselves within it. Such sessions are a good illustration of Catherine Bell's point that "ritual systems do not function to regulate or control the systems of social relations, they *are* the system" (Bell 1992: 130, emphasis in original). To develop this argument, I must explain the meaning of the Fijian term *vanua* at some length, distinguishing between its two main senses.

At its most inclusive level, *vanua* is a common noun that means both "place" and "people." It can denote a specific place—this spot, right here—or a wide territory. It can also indicate dry land as opposed to water. As "people," *vanua* refers to commoners under a chief. Sometimes this meaning is made explicit in the phrase *lewe ni vanua*, "flesh/substance of the land"; but because chiefs represent the body politic, *vanua* also means the chiefdom itself (Kaplan 1995: 27; Manoa 2010: 79; see also Tuwere 2001: 45).

The term *vanua* connotes patriarchal and self-consciously traditional values. It is prominent and pervasive in indigenous Fijian discourse, including academic, political, and religious discourse. For many Fijian Methodists, it has become an emblem of religious identity and political stance, spurring people to action at times of turmoil such as the coups of 1987 and 2000. (The coup of 2006 and its aftermath are more complicated, and are discussed in Chapter 5; an additional discussion of the increasingly polarized meanings of *vanua* follows in Chapter 6.) The land of Fiji is considered by many indigenous Fijians to be a divine gift from Jehovah to themselves. But the *vanua*, in all of its manifestations, is perpetually considered to be threatened: nonindigenous people supposedly want to take over Fijian lands; social groups are dissolving in the modern acids of money and democracy; chiefs have lost their effective power; tradition sputters and wanes. Senses of the *vanua*'s peril heighten its emotional resonance.

In short, *vanua* is both place and people, and the two sides need each other. They need each other so intimately, indeed, that they are inseparable. "For a vanua to be recognised, it must have people living on it and supporting and defending its rights and interests," according to the anthropologist turned senator Asesela Ravuvu. "A land without people is likened to a person without [a] soul" (1983: 76; see also Tuwere 2002: 35).

In Christian terms—the terms in which modern indigenous Fijian philosophy must be read—a "soul" suggests a core, a central point. This brings *vanua* into dialogue with recent Pacific scholarship on place and motion. Attempting to retheorize Oceanic territory, Vicente Diaz and Kehaulani Kauanui (referring to David Lewis) write that "islands themselves are...on the move, and if there is a stable point from which one gauges one's position, it is the canoe" (Diaz and Kauanui 2001: 317). In taking this perspective, these scholars are imaginatively inhabiting the space of Polynesian and Micronesian seafarers who began settling remote Oceania thousands of years ago.[6] They are also extending the poetic vision of Epeli Hau'ofa, who argued in a celebrated essay that scholars should think of islands as nodes on oceanic paths rather than as outposts separated by vast blank spaces (Hau'ofa 1994; see also Hau'ofa 2008, Wendt 1976).

The seagoing, motion-based perspective helps expand scholars' conceptualizations of the Pacific while highlighting the partiality and temporality of positioning (T. Teaiwa 2005). There is the suggestion of a counterpoint to this perspective, however, in indigenous emphases on genealogy and its grounded connections (Tengan, Ka'ili, and Fonoti 2010). And besides the obvious fact that many Pacific Islanders are not seafarers, for many modern indigenous Fijians, land's stable permanence is the source of its sacred nature. In other words, because land is characterized as a gift from God and a guarantee of well-being, it has an aura of immovable permanence. Accordingly, while appreciating and making use of the insights of scholars who emphasize mobile perspectives in Oceanic studies, ethnography pulls me back to shore, and here I will pay attention to land-based fixity.

The theologian and former president of the Methodist Church, Ilaitia Tuwere, writes that the *vanua* "is God's creation and gift....The histories that are lodged in each piece of land are remembered histories....Physical turfs, freighted as they are with social meanings, become partners in community-building across generations" (Tuwere 2002: 91–92; emphasis deleted). Tuwere's description of the *vanua* as "lodged" with histories and "freighted" with meanings suggests that it is first and foremost a stable, enduring site. In it, one gains the identity that grounds claims to legitimate authority. Later he adds, "The *vanua* is the womb out of which people come and into which they return. The Fijian village is often portrayed thus: *Na koro e na tu ga* (the village will always be there)" (107). Particular clans and subclans can be identified with distinct earthen house foundations (*yavu*), the ownership of which is "jealously guarded; they are passed down through the generations" (Nabobo-Baba 2006a: 110; see also Tuwere 2002: 33).[7]

Writing of her homeland in Tailevu province, Unaisi Nabobo-Baba observes that "concepts of boundary are referred to daily. The words conveying the notion of clan boundary in Vugalei are: *i yalayala* (physical land boundary), *i yatu* (social position within social structure), *i tutu* (same as *i yatu*), *i tavi* (customary role), *vanua* (geographical/physical place/spot)" (2006a: 107). Granted that boundaries are only manifest in motion—that is, through boundary-crossing—this description is not one of places that move but of places and place-based identities that stand still in fixed structures. The structures have spiritual joints, as "The Vugalei believe in spirits that guard clan boundaries.... Land houses the dead—the good and the bad spirits—so one learns early in Vugalei to treat all matters regarding land carefully" (Nabobo-Baba 2006a: 48, 81; see also Nabobo-Baba 2006b; Hocart 1912; Toren 1995).[8]

In contrast to land's fixity, people move. Each Fijian clan has a migration story explaining how they came to be where they are today, and local histories of migration articulate with a grand narrative about Fijians' origins in the lands of the Middle East. This narrative first became popular in the late nineteenth century due to Methodist missionary influence and has become widely accepted by indigenous Fijians today. Broadly, the story describes an ancestral journey from Tehran via Iraq and Ethiopia, with a period of settlement at Lake Tanganyika in East Africa. Eventually reaching the coast, the migrants built canoes, one of which was named *Kaunitoni*. Then these ancestors "sailed across the ocean, drifting eastwards towards Madagascar and South America. Places where they stopped included Papua New Guinea, New Britain and Solomon Islands" (Tuwere 2002: 23; see also France 1966; Geraghty 1977; Rokowaqa 1926; Sahlins 1962: 229). People find the story appealing for several reasons, one of which is that it gives Fijians roots in the lands of the Bible; many Fijians consider their ancestors to be "descendants of the lost tribe[s] of Israel" (Ratuva 2002: 21).

An example of a local tale of migration comes from the printed program for the opening of a new church in Baidamudamu village, Kadavu, in April 1999. It describes the travels of the ancestors of Nukunawa clan, the original landowners in the Tavuki Bay area, as follows:

Roko Seru is one of the children of Daunisai who left Verata [in Vitilevu] with one of his clan attendants to find an empty land where they could live. They rested a little bit at Rewa [also in Vitilevu] and then headed for Kadavu. They rested a little at Ono Island (Nawaisomo village) before going down the Kadavu coast when their journey reached Udulevu before anchoring the canoe and building the village of Nukunawa (Nagonedau).

When they had stayed awhile at that settlement and it was crowded because there were many clan members, Roko Tukai, the only child of Roko Seru, took a group of clan members and went to build a village at a place called Viniuniu. While at Viniuniu, they still obeyed Roko Seru at the original settlement. There were [then] many more people at Viniuniu, so they moved again to a new place called Vunidilo. Some of the members of Vunidilo village headed off and built a new dwelling-place and gave it the name Nukunuku. Later the village of Vunidilo changed its name to Baidamudamu and that has lasted until today. ([No listed author] 1999)

The practical effect of this tale's publication is to stake a claim to aboriginality and to order the ties of kinship between present-day populations. The leading chief of Nukunawa lives in Nagonedau village, next to Tavuki village, which is the seat of high chiefly power, but as the tale explains, Nukunawa also founded other villages in Tavuki Bay.

Thus the *vanua*'s mobility can be clarified as follows: as land it is stable, as people it moves. Discourse about the *vanua* is constantly in motion, circulating across a range of contexts including church services, traditional oratory, and political speeches, and is often used to conjoin *vanua*-as-place with *vanua*-as-people as tightly as possible. But these statements cannot be left at the descriptive level, for ideologies of motion (and stasis) have practical effects. Individuals might be expected to stay still: "A [Fijian] person who has the disposition of moving about continually may be asked, 'Did a rat eat your umbilical cord (that you scurry about so)?'" (Tuwere 1992: 24). More significantly, as Marshall Sahlins has demonstrated, ideologies of motion and stasis distinguish types of authority in Fiji.

Briefly, there is a classic distinction between the *vanua* as "people of the land" and chiefs, who come from the sea to take leadership of the *vanua*. Sahlins shows how relationships between land and sea, people and chiefs, are fractally recursive ones: that is, they are nested homologies in which each side reproduces the same distinctions. The chiefly "side" has its own internal distinction between chiefly and common, and the commoner "side" has the same internal distinction (see Sahlins 2004: 58–59;

I discuss fractal recursivity in Chapter 4). A paramount chief—on the chiefly side of the chiefly side, as it were—is defined by his stasis. A paramount chief " 'only sits'... receiving the offerings of the kingdom in his capacity as the human form of the gods, thus ensuring its continuity and prosperity" (Sahlins 2004: 60). In contrast, a chief associated directly with the *vanua* is defined by his motion: he "is the active king... [he] acts; he leads not only in war but in many collective works by virtue of his status as the original ruler" (60).[9]

Kava and the Sign of the Cross

Kava, called *yaqona* in Fijian, is sometimes referred to as the "water of the *vanua*" (*wai ni vanua*), a phrase that condenses its connections to both place and people. The analytical distinction between *vanua*-as-place and *vanua*-as-people lies at the crux of the chiastic structure of kava drinking. The *vanua*, like the body of Christ in communion, is what "crosses" people in kava-drinking sessions. In these sessions, people take the *vanua*-as-place into themselves as they put themselves into the *vanua*-as-people.

Kava can be identified with various locations. At the broadest level, Fijian kava is considered distinct from other national varieties, such as kava from Tonga or Vanuatu. The late Ratu Josateki Nawalowalo from Tavuki village, an enthusiastic promoter of kava's benefits, told me, "If there are two [preparations of] kava, I'm saying, two mixes of kava are there, I can know that this kava is from Vanuatu, [this other is] kava from Fiji."[10] Within Fiji, people from different regions take pride in the quality of their own kava. Shops and stalls selling kava often advertise where it has been grown, and kava from Kadavu is prominently advertised and considered high quality. Ratu Josaia Veibataki from Nagonedau village told me, "I know kava's taste. Kadavu kava has a different taste from others throughout Fiji.... The kava from other parts of Fiji is tasteless. Tasteless, and its appearance when it's mixed is, it looks bad, eh? It's not—." At this point in our conversation, his cross-cousin Mosese Naserua chimed in, "White," and Veibataki continued: "It's not nice and white, the kava's liquid is a bit red, eh? Some other kava from Kadavu [i.e., not from the Tavuki area], I can tell that it's not kava from—some kava, I can see it like this, 'oh, this is kava from Tavuki Bay' "[11] (Figure 3.1).

Even finer distinctions can be made, as some farmers give names to the varieties of kava grown in their gardens. I asked Veibataki about a variety I had heard of called "Lady Cry" (Text 3.1), and he answered:

FIGURE 3.1 Shop advertising Kadavu kava, Suva, 2011.

Text 3.1

Ratu Josaia: O, na "Lady Cry," kacei i dua ga na ila ni dua na yaqona. Dua na turaga dau teitei, na turaga ni Natumua, i vaijikojiko mai Nuku.... Iko kilai Vereti beka, Natumua?... Dau vailana tu na nona, na nona yaqona. Jiko gena na "Lady Cry." Dua gena kacei na "Wild Rose."

Ratu Josaia: Oh, "Lady Cry," that's just a name of a [kind of] kava. A farmer, a man from Natumua, has a place at Nuku.... You might know Vereti, [from] Natumua?... He gives names to his, his kava. That's the "Lady Cry." Another one is "Wild Rose."

Matt: Na dui mataqali—

Matt: Different kinds—

Ratu Josaia: Io... kena duidui mataqali, jiko ke na mataqali yaqona qaqa, e? Kia ka malumu jiko. Kia na "Wild Rose" kacei, ni iko somica, sa tautauvata jiko lako jiko i dua na loga ni rosi. Sa na tu ke na... voto ni rosi, sa na culai iko ga mai, na majeni sa na tarai iko.

Ratu Josaia: Yes... it's different kinds, there's a kind of strong kava, eh? This here [the kava we were drinking at that moment] is weak. The "Wild Rose," when you drink it, it's like you're going into a bed of roses. There will be the roses' thorns, they will pierce you, the drunkenness will get you [like that].

Matt: Au sa taura rawa.

Matt: I understand.

Ratu Josaia: Na "Lady Cry," kena ibalebale vailani ke o kia, ni iko sa somica, na ere ga sa na yacovi iko, sa na vani jiko i dua na marama, o sa na tagi jiko na gauna sa na yacova ke mai ke na majeni. Yacovi iko mai ke na majeni, e?

Ratu Josaia: "Lady Cry," the meaning of that name he gave it, when you drink it, what's going to happen to you, [you'll] be like a woman, you'll cry when the drunkenness hits you. The drunkenness hits you, eh?[12]

Matt: Vinaka, vinaka. I so tale beka na ila buli vanikacei?...

Matt: Good, thanks. Are there some other nicknames like those?...

Ratu Josaia: Io, i levu tu, e? I so dau tukuni tu na "Tabu Kaisi."

Ratu Josaia: Yes, there are lots, eh? Some people mention the "No Peasants."[13]

Matt: "Tabu Kaisi."

Matt: "No Peasants."

Ratu Josaia: Io. Kacei i so na yaqona qaqa, yaqona lelevu. Dau vani tu na "Tabu Kaisi," kena ibalebale kacei, mini je medra yaqona na kaisi, e? Medra yaqona na turaga. Kacei i dau tukuni tu na "Tabu Kaisi." Ia kacei na yaqona dina ga ni Viji, na ila dina ni yaqona ni Viji, kei na "Lady Cry," na ere kacei, na ere qai vailani vou ga ke na yaqona i na gauna ka.

Ratu Josaia: Yeah. That's some strong kava, big kava. Like the "No Peasants," its meaning is, it's not the kava for peasants to drink, eh? It's the kava for chiefs to drink. That's why it's called "No Peasants." But that's just the true Fijian kava, the true name of Fijian kava, and "Lady Cry," those things [i.e., nicknames like that], those are just newly named kava [varieties] nowadays.

At the different levels of nation, island, and garden, then, kava can have an identity based on its place of origin, like a person. As Veibataki points out, names like "Lady Cry" and "Wild Rose" are modern inventions, and it is likely that the "branding" of kava has become more detailed and site-specific as kava has become more widely commodified, part of a general trend of *vanua* branding (Pigliasco 2010). Indeed, before he passed away, Nawalowalo had big plans for a system to track kava production for brand enhancement and quality control. But local kava reputations are not a new thing. In the 1860s, Berthold Seemann noted that "Kadavu is renowned" for growing kava (Seemann 1973: 213). In 1935, when the Duke of Gloucester visited Fiji, Tavuki produced the largest root of kava to welcome his arrival: "The root was carried in triumph through the streets of Suva by a dozen men bearing a full-grown man enthroned in its centre," a cartoonishly immense size (Lester 1941: 99).

Kava can be consumed in a wide range of places: in private homes, meeting halls, makeshift outdoor pavilions (*vatunuloa*); aboard boats and ships; in the marketplace near the sign announcing that kava drinking is forbidden on the premises, and so on. It is banned in some workplaces, however, and I have never seen it drunk inside a Methodist church building. Methodists in the Tavuki Bay area drink kava every day, including Sundays after the afternoon church service, and often drink in the church social hall; but kava is never consumed within the church building itself. I return to this point later.

In ritual presentations of kava, people's identities as members of specific *vanua* are highlighted in the speeches they give and receive. During my dissertation fieldwork I lived in the house of Kadavu's superintendent minister, the Reverend Isikeli Serewai, who was a native of Ra province in Vitilevu. I was struck by how he switched into his own dialect, with its distinctive dropping of /t/ (for example, *turaga* [lord, gentleman] is pronounced *'uraga*), when giving formal speeches in which he represented his homeland. On one particularly memorable occasion at his house, in December 1998, he was visited by a medical doctor who came from Natewa in Cakaudrove province, where speakers drop /k/. I marveled, as the doctor presented the minister with kava and the churchman reciprocated with a whale's tooth, that we were sitting here in Kadavu and the speech around me, rolling in ceremonial timbres but pitted with dropped consonants, indexed the two *vanua* of Ra and Cakaudrove.[14]

In any kava-drinking session, whether formal or casual, a ritual structure is consistently followed. I have discussed this elsewhere (see Tomlinson 2009: 112–114) and here cover only the major points here as they relate to chiasmus. People are generally seated in a roughly round or oval shape, with higher-ranked drinkers sitting farther from the bowl ("above," *icake* in Fijian) and lower-ranked drinkers, including those doing the work of preparing and serving the kava, sitting closer to the bowl and behind it ("below," *ira*). Those sitting below the bowl can cluster informally. When women are present, they often sit in their own group to the side of the central male drinking group.[15] Methodist ministers generally sit "high" in the hierarchy but not as high as leading chiefs. The serving of cups follows a hierarchical order which, in Tavuki, begins with the highest-ranked person present.[16] The second cup goes to the *matanivanua* (*vanua*'s representative, or herald, who acts as the master of ceremonies, calling for new rounds of drinking). After that, cups are generally served according to the seating pattern (see Figure 3.2).

When chiefs are present, their status is reinforced by the way they are served. They sit "highest," drink before others, often use their own cups, and speak authoritatively during discussions. Traditionally, a chief is supposed to receive the ability to speak effectively by being formally installed in his position with a kava ceremony: "Once he has drunk the chiefly yaqona his every command must be fulfilled on pain of his mystical power causing illness to those who fail to do their duty" (Toren 1999: 33). As

FIGURE 3.2 Kava-drinking session, Nagonedau, Kadavu, 2006.

Sahlins notes, the classic Fijian ritual installation of a chief involved killing him symbolically by serving him kava:

> At his own accession the Fijian chief is symbolically poisoned, and
> in this way captured and domesticated as a god of the indigenous
> people. The poison is in the sacred offering, the drink made from
> the kava plant that consecrates the chief. Kava is the preeminent
> offering of the ancient *lewe ni vanua,* "members of the land," to the
> ruling chief, always himself a foreigner by origin. Myth tells that
> kava first grew from the dead body of a child or young chief of the
> native people.... The stranger-king thus consumes the land and
> appropriates its reproductive powers, but only to suffer thereby his
> own appropriation. (Sahlins 1985: 75)

In this model, chiefs and the *vanua*—people of the land, who will become
the subjects of the chiefdom—stand in a relationship of chiasmus to each
other. The subjects present kava to the chief so he can symbolically take
control of them and their land; in doing so, the *vanua* kills him, taking
control of his power over them. As Sahlins notes, this is a double movement of appropriation. The ritual logic is watertight, although in present-
day Kadavu (and apparently in many other place in Fiji) local disputes
mean that chiefs are often not installed any more.

The structure of kava drinking is evident even in the most casual
circles. A kava session is never a free-for-all: even if it is just a group of
friends drinking to relax, floating through the afternoon cup by pleasant
cup, a definite order of service is followed from first served to last served,
with clapping and the utterance of "empty" (*maca*) at appropriate times.
Part of a session's orderliness comes from the formulaic announcements
that always begin it and finish it. At the beginning, before anyone has
drunk, two announcements are given: one after the kava has been crushed
into powder ("The kava has been pounded"), and one after the first bowl
has been mixed ("The kava is clear"). At the end, a final announcement is
made to declare that the session is finished ("The kava is empty"), although
people sometimes continue drinking after this point. Following each
of these announcements, the herald gives a one-word response ("mix"
after the first announcement, "clap" after the second two; see Tomlinson
2009: 112).

Like all rituals, kava drinking is prone to disruptions and challenges.
At a trivial level, people might sit in a place that others think they do

not belong; that is, they might sit too high for that session. (It is more common for people to sit too low and gradually to be coaxed into sitting in a more appropriate, higher place.) A more significant challenge is to refuse to participate: if a man does not attend kava sessions, he can cut himself off from much of village life. This is notably the case with members of religious groups that forbid kava drinking. Many evangelical Christian denominations ban it for at least two reasons. One is that kava can make a person "drunk," relaxed to the point of extreme wobbliness, and excessive drinking can cause a kind of hangover (Aporosa 2013).[17] Because some drinking sessions go into the early hours of the morning, too, people might sleep late and get less work done the next day. The second reason is that kava is associated with non-Christian ancestors. Drinking alone is considered sorcery, a way to communicate with wicked spirits. More generally, the act of drinking kava, even within groups, is thought to establish a connection with dangerous spiritual forces.

One evangelical Christian, a highly ranked chief and a leading official at the Kadavu Provincial Office, told me in January 2006 that the ritual announcements made at the beginning and end of each kava-drinking session were speech acts that summoned demons (Text 3.2).

In Banivalu's view, the formulaic announcements that begin every kava session are really demonic invitations. Not surprisingly, Methodists disagree with the idea that kava drinking is inherently evil; for them, drinking is a primary means of social interaction, a way to honor kin ties and build new relationships, to attend to chiefs and organize the working life of the village. Many Methodists attend church faithfully and support their ministers, many of whom participate enthusiastically in kava drinking themselves. And yet some of the evangelical distrust has crept in: one Methodist minister told me that he offered prayers aloud at kava-drinking sessions because participants may have been silently serving devils there (see Tomlinson 2009: 127–128).

Previously, I stated that chiasmus defines the pattern of kava-drinking sessions' ritual acts of incorporation: people take the *vanua* (as place) into themselves by drinking it, thereby putting themselves into the *vanua* (as people). Moving in this X-shaped pattern, I suggested, people make themselves belong to a place and to other people in a marked, definite way: a hierarchical order with inflections of chiefly, religious, and secular authority. Whereas the body of Christ is the term that "crosses" participants in holy communion, the *vanua* is the term that "crosses" participants in

Ratu Jona Banivalu: Na yaqona na iyaragi dina ni kai Viti ni se bera ni cabe na lotu.

Ratu Jona Banivalu: Kava was the true weapon of Fijians before Christianity came here.

Matt: Vinaka. Ia i na gauna sa [mai] rarama [tu] o Viji, na nomu vakasama beka, na nomu vabauta, [sa] dodonu me tabu na somi yaqona.

Matt: Thanks. But when Fiji was converted, it's your thought, it's your belief, that kava should not be drunk [anymore].

Ratu Jona: Io. Baleta ni sa biu na tevoro, e? Koya a nodra kalou jiko mai me biu vata kei na kena iyaya me da kua ni kauta vata kei na Kalou oqo. Kevaka o sa via qarava na Kalou oqo, mo masu ga, tekivu na bose... .

Ratu Jona: Yes. Because the devils were rejected, eh? The gods they [the ancestors] had should be rejected along with their possessions/objects so we don't bring them to this [Christian] God. If you want to serve this God, just pray [to] begin a meeting... .

Matt: Vinaka.

Matt: Thanks.

Ratu Jona: Io. Oqo, ni sa dau caka jiko na, ka, ni sa dau vakarau tekivu na bose, caka mada na isevusevu. A caka na isevusevu. Oji ya, o iko sa qai kacivaka jiko, "Sa vutu kora tu na yaqona." O iko kacivaka jiko vei cei?

Ratu Jona: Right. Here, when a, when a meeting is ready to begin, a *isevusevu* [ceremonial presentation of kava between guests and hosts] is performed. The *isevusevu* is performed. After that, you call out, "The kava has been pounded." Who are you calling out to?

Matt: Vei kedra na turaga sa [mai] dabe jiko?

Matt: To the chiefs who are sitting there?

Ratu Jona: Ia na cava o kacivaka jiko icake ni na raica jiko ga?

Ratu Jona: But why call it out loud when you can just see them?

Matt: Kerekere, mo vakamacalatakina mada ga vei au.

Matt: Please, explain it to me.

Ratu Jona:...Nĭo kacivaka gona, e? Nĭo kacivaka, kena ibalebale, e dua tani tale na ka o iko via kaciva. Baleta o ira na tevoro, e na gauna sa qaravi kina, o ira na kacivi, e? Me rawa na vakila sa varau tekivu oqo e dua na ka. Sa na kacivaki, me rawa na lako mai me ra na mai wawa e tau tuba.

Ratu Jona:...When you call like that, eh? When you call it out, its meaning is that there's something else you want to announce. Because the devils, when they were worshiped [in the old days], they were called, eh? So they would know that something was about to begin. They would be called so they could come and wait outside.

Matt: Oi.

Ratu Jona: E?

Matt: Uh.

Ratu Jona: "Sa vutu kora tu na yaqona."...Sa kacivaka mai, "Bali." O ira sa na cici mai ya. "Sa darama tu na yaqona." Ya na ka a dau caka e liu. Ni sa vakarau ni gunu na bete, o ira sa tu ituba. O koya na qai kaciva, "Kalou ni cava o iratou vinakata na turaga?" Kevaka eratou vinakata me taroga na ivalu, o koya na kaci ga ni ituba vua na kalou ni valu, e na taroga na bete. Koya, oya e kacivaki jiko na yaqona, me kacivaki jiko icake.

Matt: Oh.

Ratu Jona: Eh?

Matt: Uh.

Ratu Jona: "The kava has been pounded."..."Mix" is called out. Then they come running. "The kava is clear." That's how it was done before [in the old days]. When the priest was getting ready to drink [kava], they [the devils] stood outside. He would call out, "What god do you chiefs want?" If they wanted to ask about [the prospects for] war, the priest would call outside to the god of war to ask him questions. There, that's why when kava is announced, it's said aloud [like that].[18]

---

kava-drinking sessions. Seen in this way, kava drinking might be called the communion of the *vanua*.

Evangelicals who reject kava drinking might thus seem to be putting themselves outside the orbit of the *vanua*. This is how I first interpreted the situation, although, after further consideration, I realize it is more insightful to analyze the ways in which evangelical practice itself distinguishes between *vanua*-as-place and *vanua*-as-people. Nicholas Thomas writes of an observation he made in western Vitilevu, "Nothing seemed more pathetic than the sight of an individual Seventh-day Adventist sitting with a glass of water on the periphery of a kava circle" (Thomas 1997: 50). I would suggest that rather than being pathetic, this shows both the pull of the *vanua* and its remarkable accommodation. The Adventist man evidently wanted to have a presence in village social life, even if he was marginalized, and the drinkers did not exclude him. Similarly, in Tavuki, one middle-aged man who had joined an evangelical sect occasionally did this sort of thing—he attended kava-drinking sessions and participated in aspects of the ritual (even calling out approval of others' drinking) without consuming kava himself. Practically speaking, what evangelical Christians do in rejecting kava drinking is insist that kava does not unite the *vanua* with Jehovah but, rather, separates the two. They do not necessarily accept the sacredness of ancestral land, which in their view is infested with devils

Text 3.3

Lotu ni Kavitu...e doka vakalevu sara na itovo vakavanua, a, na ivakarau ni veiwekani, a, na bula vakaitikotiko, na veiqaravi vakavanua eso era, era doka vakalevu ena veivanua era tu kina ka era oka vakalewenivanua. Ia mai na nodra rai ni vakabauta a vakayavutaki vakaivolatabu, e so na ivalavala vakavanua me vaka na somi yaqona, a, taralala, na meke—e so na i, na itovo era taurivaki ka tiki ni gacagaca ni veiqaravi vakavanua, a, na Lotu ni Kavitu era sega ni dau vakaitavitaki ira kina. Sega ni kena ibalebale oqo ni ra sega ni tiko ena soqo.	Seventh-day Adventism...very strongly respects *vanua* customs, the kinship system, community life, some services for the *vanua* they respect very much wherever they are and they are counted as members of the *vanua*. But from their beliefs based in the Bible, some of the *vanua* practices like drinking kava, dancing, the *meke*—some of the, the customs that are practiced, part of the service to the *vanua*, Seventh-day Adventists do not take part in them. This does not mean that they are not present at gatherings.

and in dire need of spiritual cleansing. But this does not mean that they want to be cut off from their kin, as a Seventh-day Adventist minister, Timoci Beitaki, told me in June 2009 (Text 3.3).

The minister's implication—you can participate in the life of the *vanua* by being present at events like kava sessions while not actually drinking kava—leads to a final consideration of kava and communion. When I have asked Fijian Methodists over the years about the possibility of using kava instead of wine as a sacred Christian element, the response has been overwhelmingly negative, as Ratu Josaia Veibataki told me (Text 3.4).

Veibataki implies that the paths of *lotu* (Christianity) and the *vanua* are distinct: one uses wine for the former and kava for the latter, and for worship one should only follow the path of Christianity. Many indigenous Fijians would agree heartily with his argument. Indeed, as I noted at the beginning of this chapter, Jovili Meo argued as a theology student in 1973 that Methodist communion needed "a more Fijian order which is more meaningful to us, and this means the renewal of the whole structure," but despite calling for a more Fijian order he did not take the step of suggesting that kava be used instead of wine. Instead, he suggested only that communicants sit *as if* they were at a kava-drinking session, and that vessels used to serve kava be used to serve wine.

Text 3.4

Noqu nanuma baleta na, na waini ma se—kena inaki ga kia ka, e? Kia ka taurivaki jiko ke i Viji i na gauna ni davu, vatakarakara jiko ke na ere i tukuni jiko na Ivola Tabu na, na waini, e? Baleta ka i duidui jiko na yaqona ni Viji, e?...Baleta na yaqona ni Viji, dau vayagataki tu tale i mada, me dra dau wai ni qaravi kalou vu na qase. I, kena ibalebale, i na mini rawa ni vayagataki na, na yaqona ni kalou vu vua na...Kalou levu keda qarava jiko ni davu, e? Ke dua i—se vayagatakina na, na yaqona ki na nona qaravi lotu, kacei sa tautauvata jiko sa vajimoni jiko, e?

My thought about the, the wine was—this was its purpose, eh? This is its use in Fiji today, in the Bible wine is said to be a symbol, eh? Because Fijian kava is different, eh?...Because Fijian kava was also used by the ancestors in olden days as the water for worshiping ancestral spirits. This means it would be impossible to use the ancestral spirits' kava for the...great God we worship today, eh? If someone is still using kava in his worship, that's the same as demonism, eh?

A year later, another Fijian student repeated Meo's suggestion, acknowledging Meo's influence and mentioning that a faculty member at the Pacific Theological College, John Garrett, had provided "guidance and help" in testing alternative communion arrangements (Curulala 1974: 64). In the early 1990s, another student observed that kava "can be almost like a sacrament" (Vakadewavosa 1991: 75). A master's degree candidate laid out the issues thoroughly in 1994, referring to kava's "sacramental character" and going so far as to call kava an "element," the term used for the substances consumed in Christian communion. He called attention to the motion of chiasmus that I have outlined, noting the similarity between Paul's metaphor of the church as the body of Christ and kava's relationship with the *vanua*. After drawing these criss-crossing lines, however, he did not go on to say that kava might actually be used in a church service for communion (see Kuru 1994: 61–63).

Within Fiji there is one spectacular artistic representation of kava as a Christian substance: Jean Charlot's mural (Figure 3.3), painted in a Catholic church near Rakiraki in the early 1960s, depicting Christ on the cross with kava plants growing behind him and a kava bowl near his feet.[19] And, finally, there is at least one Fijian Methodist leader who endorses the idea of using kava in Christian communion. I interviewed the theologian and former church president Ilaitia Tuwere in Auckland in July 2007 and

FIGURE 3.3 Jean Charlot's "Black Christ" with kava bowl, Navunibitu, Ra, 2009.

asked him if it would be acceptable to use kava in a sacramental manner. He responded:

Ah, no problem for me, no problem for me. I have tried it in Fiji. We were talking about this in the theological college when we were young, in the Pacific Theological College. But, you know, the Fijian world was—cosmos was broken when the church arrived, when missionaries arrived, and we have been trying to get back to it, and it's not easy. When I tried this *yaqona* in holy communion, ho, it was not very easy—I mean, people walked out! [Laughs] Not in the church, we did [it at] a conference... not in the church building. I was not, it was not—it would be stupid to do it in the church, in the first place in the church. But just to try it out in the conference, we were talking. But not only for me, we had been talking about this all this time. But I think it wouldn't be right to impose ideas on others if they don't accept it. Even if it's all right or, you know, even if you see that this is OK, but I think it would be wrong if you impose ideas on others when they are not ready to accept it. [Laughs] But for me... I don't have problems with that.

But on that, I would like to add that *yaqona*... is called *wai ni vanua, wai ni vanua*, water of the land, *yaqona*. When a chief is installed, you know, to become a chief, he is given the *wai ni vanua*—the whole ceremony.... Somewhere there, the kingmakers will give him the *wai ni vanua. Wai ni vanua* is—when he drinks it, he is drinking the whole *vanua* into himself, so that after that, he is no longer himself: he becomes the embodiment of the *vanua...* .

So he is no longer just an individual standing up there. He becomes the meeting point of all the people in his *matanitu* [polity]. Not only people, but also the meeting point of the seas and the rivers and the mountains, when he is being installed, after being installed. And this is the significance of *wai ni vanua, wai ni vanua*. Water is [a] symbol of life, and *vanua* is the whole land.[20]

Tuwere acknowledges that people might be "not ready to accept" the use of kava in communion, and he observes more generally that reviving tradition is difficult because the "Fijian...cosmos was broken" by Christian missionaries in the nineteenth century. He is not personally opposed to the idea, however, and he appeals to the classic model of chiefly installation in which the chief drinks kava in order to become a "meeting point"— the middle of the X. Subjects' control over their chief, and his control over them as well as "the seas and the rivers and the mountains," is condensed and conjoined in the cup of kava the chief drinks at installation.

But this kind of conjunction, I have argued, is seen in every kava-drinking session, even the most informal ones. Even when people are simply enjoying a bowl of Lady Cry on a slow evening with a small group of friends, kava drinking is a form of communion. Both Christian communion and Fijian kava drinking follow the logic of chiasmus, conjoining two elements that cross each other in incorporation. In the case of kava-drinking sessions, as people take the *vanua* into themselves, they put themselves into the *vanua*. But while kava and communion are formally similar in this way, they diverge from each other at a higher level in which the possibility of conjunction is refused, not celebrated. In Christian communion, Fijian participants incorporate themselves in a church that transcends the *vanua*; in kava drinking, they incorporate themselves in the *vanua* in a way that some believe threatens to take them away from the church.

4

Happy Deaths Are Public Deaths

*It is a consoling fact to the Missionary in Fiji, that,
although the light of the Gospel is not very steadily reflected
from the lives of many of the members, yet, in numbers of
instances it shines clearly forth upon their dying beds.*

THE REVEREND A. J. WEBB, WESLEYAN MISSIONARY
NOTICES, 1870[1]

IN THIS CHAPTER, I analyze nineteenth-century Methodist missionary
reports from Fiji that focus on "happy deaths," deathbed scenes in which
dying converts indicate that they are going to heaven. I draw on Michael
Warner's provocative definition of a public as a product of textual circulation, or "a space of discourse organized by nothing other than discourse
itself....[A public] exists by virtue of being addressed" (Warner 2002: 67;
emphasis deleted). As described in Chapter 1, the category of "public" is
configured against the category of "private" in a *fractally recursive* pattern
of entextualization, a co-constitutive distinction that "can be reproduced
repeatedly by projecting it onto narrower and broader comparisons"
(Gal 2005: 27). Here, I analyze the public-private division in relation to
another fractally recursive pair, that of life and death. I argue that missionaries aimed to create reading publics back home by circulating published
accounts of happy deaths, building global Christendom with the stories
of converts who had left heathenism behind to find Christ at their bed-
side in their final moments of life. However, the missionaries' attempts to
reshape indigenous Fijians' visions of the afterlife created a new, private
space for the demonic, a restricted sphere for talk about evil beings who
haunt Christian Fiji to this day.

As Susan Gal notes, in fractal recursivity "calibrations are always relative positions"; terms like public and private, and life and death, are defined against each other and are "not properties laminated onto the persons, objects, or spaces concerned" (2002: 81).[2] But because fractally recursive terms are also indexes—signs whose relationship is defined by physical or causal connection—they can be "difficult to discuss explicitly. Once named and thus semanticized, the fleeting distinctions of different roles, spaces, and categories indexically invoked in interaction turn into reified 'objects' of the social world that seem solid and distinct" (Gal 2002: 85; see also Gal 2005; Gal and Woolard 2001). As a result of their condensation and objectification, she argues, these are creative signs that can be used as especially powerful tools for transforming social relationships. She gives the example of Hungarian government planners who had to endorse the state's emphasis on public agency and responsibility but also wanted to inject opportunities for private economic activity. They created a private realm partly by calling it a public one, using "the fractal possibilities of the public/private distinction [as] a resource and template for conceptualizing and then creating social change. Importantly... the embedding itself allowed [the Hungarian planners] to deny that anything really drastic had been done" (2002: 90).

With the distinction between life and death, too, fine calibrations can have forceful consequences. As noted in Chapter 1, some living people are fully alive, and some dead people are fully dead, but some of the living are considered already dead, and some of the dead are more lively than others. A classic ethnographic example comes from Evans-Pritchard's account of tragic Gatbuogh:

> There was living in a village [in western Nuerland] an unhappy-looking man of unkempt appearance, called Gatbuogh. This man had some years before gone on a distant journey and had not been heard of for a long time. Then there came to his village news of his death and in course of time the mortuary ceremony was held for him. He later returned home and was living in the village at the time of my visit. He was described as *joagh in tegh*, the living ghost. I was told... "his soul was cut off. His soul went with the soul of the (sacrificed) ox together. His flesh alone remains standing." His soul, the essential part of him, had gone and with it his social personality. Although people fed him

he seems to have lost such privileges of kinship as pertain to the living and not to the dead. I was told that he could not partake of sacrificial meat because his agnatic kinship (*buth*) had been obliterated (*woc*) by the mortuary ceremony. A neighbour said to me "he lives in our village with Baranyai but we do not count him a member of it because he is dead. The mortuary ceremony has been held for him." (1956: 152–153)

The neighbor's remarkable assertion that Gatbuogh "lives in our village...[but] he is dead" illustrates the peculiar dynamics of life and death as fractally related terms. He is both alive and dead, but with different consequences entailed by each judgment: alive enough to be given food, dead enough to be cut off from his kin.

Just as biologically living people can be classified as socially dead, so too can biologically dead people have a lively social existence. For example, describing late-antiquity Christian martyrs as "the very special dead," Peter Brown writes: "They had died in a special way; they lay in the grave in a special way; this fact was shown by the manner in which all that was most delightful and most alive in late-antique life could be thought of as concentrated in their tombs and even...in detached fragments of their dead bodies" (1981: 70–71). The martyrs were "very special" because they were a species of living dead. Most Christian visions of the living dead are not so pleasant, of course: they feature eerie, predatory monstrosities like bloated vampires, shape-shifting ghosts, and troops of zombies carrying out the hidden work of capitalism (see, respectively, Barber 1988; Gordillo 2004: 209–211; and Comaroff and Comaroff 1999, Geschiere 1997).

Boundaries between fractally recursive categories are never finally fixed but pushed one way and pulled the other. Methodist missionaries in nineteenth-century Fiji, by paying close attention—almost obsessive attention—to people's deathbeds, turned them into sites of performance in which the work of pushing and pulling got done. In doing so, missionaries helped reshape relationships between Fijians' own categories of life (*bula*) and death (*mate*), and also the way those categories were configured in public and private circulation. Happy deaths became public deaths, deathbed scenes that appealed to Christian readers overseas who could participate vicariously as the missionaries fulfilled Christ's "Great Commission" to "teach all nations...to observe all things whatsoever

I have commanded you: and lo, I am with you alway, even unto the end of the world" (Matthew 28:19–20). Locally, however, missionaries' narratives of the afterlife displaced Fijian ancestors into a new demonic realm, and narratives of death relating to this demonic realm now follow a privatized circulation pattern.

Learning to "Fall Asleep in Jesus"

The pioneering Methodist missionaries in Fiji worked under the auspices of the Wesleyan Methodist Missionary Society, based in London. When the first British missionaries arrived on Fijian shores in 1835, they encountered death rituals and beliefs in spiritual afterlives that were richly elaborated.

One of the earliest and fullest descriptions was published by Thomas Williams. "When the hour of death is allowed to approach naturally," he wrote, "the dying man mentions his foe, that his children may perpetuate his hatred...and kill him at the first opportunity. The name of the hated one is uttered aloud, if not as the object of immediate vengeance, yet of gloomy and disastrous predictions" (1982 [1858]: 186–187; see also Deane 1921: 41–42). In other words, a person's dying words were meant to be an enemy's death sentence as well. But words were not the only signs that one manipulated on one's deathbed: death, for men and women alike, was often something to be dressed for in the proper way. Men's bodies were washed, oiled, painted, covered in fine barkcloth, and topped with "a clean head-dress"; women's bodies were oiled and given new skirts, "their heads dressed and ornamented," and their faces and chests coated with turmeric powder (Williams 1982 [1858]: 188, 189).

Preparations for death were based partly in beliefs that the *yalo*, which would come to be translated as "soul," could grow "too weak to sustain life" even when a person was still walking, talking, and breathing (Toren 1998: 97). As a result, one could anticipate death and act accordingly: "To recognize for oneself that one's life was no longer viable allowed one to seize control of one's own death and direct the obsequies, even where that death had been initiated by others" (97). The treatment of dying bodies did not please the missionaries, who were disturbed by a sense of prematurity. "The process of laying out [the body]," Williams observed grimly, "is often commenced several hours before the person is actually dead" (1982 [1858]: 188; see also Wallis 1983 [1851]: 265–266). The missionaries faced a version of what we might call Gatbuough's dilemma: they saw people being treated as dead when, in British terms, they were still very much alive.

Besides being disturbed by premature death preparations, the missionaries were bothered by the ritual logic in which one death often precipitated others, not only through deathbed curses but also because wives and companions of chiefs were sometimes sacrificed when chiefs died. As Williams explained, "the idea of a Chieftain going into the world of spirits unattended, is most repugnant to the native mind" (1982 [1858]: 188). Missionaries expressed shock and amazement when chiefly wives went obediently to their deaths, usually strangled by their kin.[3]

In seeking to understand Fijian attitudes toward death, Williams argued that people believed "in an eternal existence" without having "the idea of any moral retribution in the shape either of reward or punishment" (1982 [1858]: 243). In other words, the realm of death was simply another land, another place generally called Bulu and incorporating the paradise of Burotu (see Chapter 3, note 7). The path to this otherworld was drawn in great narrative detail, full of tests and battles for the deceased. Basil Thomson summarized the path through the afterlife as follows:

> Though the story of the Soul's journey agreed in general outline, the details were filled in by each tribe to suit its geographical position. There was generally water to cross, either the sea or a river, and there was, therefore, a ghostly ferryman (Vakaleleyalo) who treated his passengers with scant courtesy. There was Ghost-scatterer, who stoned the Shade, and Reed-spear, who impaled him. Goddesses of fearsome aspect peered at him, gnashing their teeth; the god of murder fell upon him; the Dismisser sifted out the real dead from the trance-smitten; fisher-fiends entangled cowards in their net; at every turn in the road there was some malevolent being to put the Shade to the ordeal, and search out every weak point, until none but brave warriors who had died a violent death—the only sure passport to [Burotu]—passed through unscathed. (1968 [1908]: 117; see also Thomson 1895; Waterhouse 1997 [1866]: 290–296)

Methodist missionaries were scandalized by such narratives. They were offended by the polytheism, violence, and gore, and the audacious claims of traditional priests who were Christian evangelists' direct competitors for religious authority (Thornley 2002). A typically uncharitable characterization came from David Cargill, one of the first two British missionaries in Fiji, who dismissed the whole complex religion of indigenous Fiji as a "system of lies" (1977: 75).

As Vicente Rafael (1988: 187) writes of Spanish Catholic missionaries' focus on Tagalogs' deathbeds in the Philippines, "On the threshold of loss, tensions between Christian and pagan beliefs and practices tended to be played out most explicitly." For this reason, missionaries were encouraged to understand local beliefs about the afterlife in order to guard against "pagan contamination" of Catholic practice; and because priests often could not make it to the deathbed in time, local auxiliaries were expected to ensure that people died well. One priest even "recommended that 'responsible persons' in the village be provided with 'some guide or little book' containing the necessary formula to help the dying achieve a 'good death'" (187). Similarly for Methodist missionaries in Fiji, deathbeds were chosen as a primary site of engagement, a place to replace the "system of lies" with truth and a newly disciplined way of dying.

The actions taking place at Christian deathbeds, both in the Catholic Philippines and Methodist Fiji, show how ritual can be seen as "less about giving voice to shared values than about opening fields of argument; about providing the terms and tropes...through which people caught up in changing worlds may vex each other, question definitions of value, form alliances, and mobilize oppositions" (Comaroff and Comaroff 1993: xxiii). In the cases I will examine, deaths prompted two kinds of ritual action. The first was simply a rite of passage in which the dying person, often in dialogue with a missionary, attended carefully to his or her own words and actions in order to both ensure and prove that he or she was going to Heaven. The second ritual act was the entextualization of these deaths in mission publications in regularly patterned ways, namely, in generic narratives.

Missionaries looked for "good deaths" or "happy deaths" not only for the benefit of people in Fiji, but also for reading publics back home in places like England and Australia. The missionaries built on textual traditions of the previous century. Alan Tippett, describing the nineteenth-century Wesleyans in Fiji, wrote that "they left the record of scores of triumphal deathbed scenes which might have come out of 18th century Wesleyanism" (1976: 118), and these narratives were probably built on earlier British genres such as the accounts of gallows-bound criminals' confessions and their "last dying speeches," published popularly in a series from the 1670s until the 1770s (McKenzie 2003: 171). In addition, by the early nineteenth century, British "royal deaths were seen as a very public affair," with, for example, "Princess Charlotte's last agony... narrated in detail in commemorative pamphlets" in 1817 (Wolffe 2000: 19).[4]

The deathbed scenes reported by Methodist missionaries from Fiji are generic, but they vary considerably in their length and details. I believe I have located the shortest possible account: Alfred J. Collocott's 1882 circuit report for Kadavu records a man's passing away at Drue village in two words, "Good death."

Other reports are longer, of course, and they usually indicate the missionaries' deep concern with linguistic evidence of good Christians' inner states. As Webb Keane has argued, for "modern" Protestant subjects spiritual authority is grounded in an imagined interior state marked by morally laden attributes (e.g., sincerity or insincerity) that are revealed through language (Keane 2002; see also Keane 2006, 2007). To a significant extent, Fijian converts were being taught that to die the right way meant to speak the right way, revealing the state of their souls in all sincerity. Here are three examples:

> We have met with very cheering testimonies from those who have fallen asleep in Jesus. They speak in very confident terms of their inheritance in heaven. (Nolan 1896)

> We have been greatly encouraged by the large number of happy deaths that have taken place in our midst, not only have they given clear testimony that they knew they were going to be with Jesus... but in some instances before they launched away they were permitted to see visions of the eternal world, and with faces reflecting the light of the glory land, they have told their watching friends of beckoning angels and words of welcome which their ears only were permitted to hear. These happy deaths have had a beneficial effect upon us as a church, and have led many to say, "Let me die the death of the righteous, and let my last end be like his." (Allen 1892)

> It is always a source of great joy to us when we know that our members, as they pass away into the eternal world, leave a bright testimony that they have ["]gone to be for ever with the Lord." A chief of a small town near the Mission Station died happily in Jesus the other day. Shortly before his spirit soared on high to the home of the blessed, he said, when asked with regard to his prospect of the future—"The Spirit of God bears witness with my spirit that I am

a child of GOD." "Every day I feel a desire to be with Jesus. I rejoice that I possess the religion that saves my soul, for I know that the day my body returns to the dust my spirit will pass away to GOD.["] Many poor Fijians, once numbered amongst Adam's most degraded and polluted sons[,] have been saved through faith in the atonement of Jesus, and are now with those who have entered upon an eternal rest. (White 1867a)

In each of these accounts, the key word is *testimony*—a speech act in which the soon-to-be-deceased subjects speak as authoritative witnesses of their own salvation in Christian terms. In all three of these cases, the missionaries evidently approve of dying Fijians' utterances and diagnose local deaths as happy ones. Nolan observes people's confidence, Allen admires their clarity, and White applies the common trope of brightness or light in Christian accounts of happy deaths to the words of his subjects: "our members...leave a bright testimony."

For the missionaries, testimonies of happy deaths were the kinds of texts whose circulation could help form a Christian reading public back home. But in selecting (or, more likely, co-constructing) these texts as exemplary, the missionaries set in motion an intriguing dynamic: if a happy death is proven by utterance of the "right" words, then indigenous Fijians, not white missionaries, are the ones who represent their own fate. Sometimes dying subjects offered commentary on their own words, suggesting that they recognized the signs that would galvanize other Christians and, perhaps, draw effective boundaries for a new Christian public. For example, Frederick Langham gave the following account of the death of a young boy named Luke Toroca: "When dying [he] said 'Father send for my namesake and for vugoqu [my niece or nephew] that I may speak to them as I am dying.'" After saying farewell, the boy "cried aloud 'Eternal life! Eternal life! Eternal life!' and then his happy spirit 'soared away to the realms of light + blessedness to eternal life in the bright world above'" (Langham n.d.: 108). Toroca, only eight or nine years old in Langham's estimation, was aware (at least as Langham reports the scene) that his words were weighted with particular pragmatic force because he was dying and moving into a Christian afterlife. The young boy accepts his early death but insists on being able to speak to his relatives as he lies dying in order to demonstrate the happiness of his death.

In another case, a dying man was particularly concerned with how people would speak of his death after its occurrence:

> In January last one of our most valuable Catechists in this Circuit died, and showed the power of religion over death, in a most delightful manner. Rapid consumption weakened his body; but as his mortal frame grew weaker, his faith appeared to increase. A few hours before his death, he said to his friends who stood around him, "When I am gone, do not say I am *dead,* but only *removed;*" using a native word which signifies "moving from one residence to another." He then quoted 2 Corinthians v. 1; and soon after closed his eyes on this world, to add one more to the increasing number of redeemed and saved natives around the throne of God. (Polglase 1858: 26)[5]

Like the young boy Luke Toroca, the catechist attempted to manage his death through speech which, in this case, was also meant to shape others' speech after he was gone (see also Murray 1888: 95). The scene is presented joyfully: what could be better, in Christian terms, than denying the finality of physical death ("do not say I am dead"), quoting the Bible, and affirming and perpetuating the rightness of missionary teachings?[6]

Indeed, models of happy deaths could inspire the living, teaching them how they ought to die in the future. Jesus's death is one model: "Christ is thought to figure the perfect fusion of appearance and essence, contingency and necessity, loss and gain. To die beautifully thus amounts to miming his death in that it entails the conversion of one's fear of loss into a sign of one's surrender to the Father" (Rafael 1988: 207). Within Fiji, one of the best-known historical examples concerns the missionary John Hunt, who, as he lay dying, "Repeatedly... broke out in prayer, 'Lord, bless Fiji! Save Fiji! Thou knowest my soul has loved Fiji: my heart has travailed in pain for Fiji!'" (Birtwhistle 1954: 144–145). Fiji's dominant chief of the mid- and late nineteenth century, Ratu Seru Cakobau, "did not [convert] for some years after this event, but in later life he used to say that the dying prayer of Hunt was the beginning of his conversion" (Birtwhistle 1954: 144–145). Later, he "confessed that he was 'favourably impressed towards the Christian religion, when I saw it made dying not only easy but triumphant'" (Tippett 1954: 16; see also Nettleton 1906: 114–117; Thornley 2000: 441). When his own death approached, Ratu Cakobau displayed Hunt's influence:

A day or two before [Ratu Cakobau's] death he said to one of his attendants, "Faith is a good thing, it is a great thing, for it is by faith we are saved. Ah, Salvation is a great thing. Salvation is the one thing." Towards the middle of the night before his death he said, "We have not had prayers yet, have we? Well, we will have them now, and I will conduct them," and then he prayed in his usual beautifully simple style. The name of Jesus was often on his lips, and to those around him he would say, "Be thou faithful unto death." Once he prayed, "Lord, be gracious unto me. Here I lie in obedience to Thy will. Life and death are in Thy hands. Thou alone rulest." Early in the morning of the day on which he died, he was heard praying, "Lord, be gracious to Thy servant. Help me this day. Give me Thy Holy Spirit, for the sake of Jesus Thy Son, my Saviour." His last audible prayer was, "Hold me, Jesus! Hold me, Jesus! My faith in Thee is firm." And thus passed away the King of Fiji, a trophy of divine grace. (Reed 1888: 77–78)

In his dying words, the chief effectively responded to the lessons John Hunt had taught decades earlier. Hunt had prayed that Fiji be saved; Ratu Cakobau, who embodied the collectivity of Fijians in his role as leading chief, enacted this salvation on his deathbed. Where the minister had prayed, "Lord, bless Fiji! Save Fiji!" the chief had responded, "salvation is a great thing. Salvation is the one thing." It is almost as if he were completing a speech act begun by Hunt thirty years before.[7]

Another likely audience for happy deaths was the ancestors who were being dismissed by being conspicuously ignored. In other words, to the extent that missionaries believed Fijian ancestral spirits existed, they might have seen happy deaths as performances telling these spirits that they were no longer welcome. In some Fijian villages, spirits were explicitly bade farewell, told directly that their people were now Christian (see, e.g., Thornley 2002: 343).

Dying with confidence is recommended in the Fijian Methodist catechism, a set of questions and answers appended to the hymnal. Under the topic of "Death and the Life to Come," one of the questions is, "Is it good that we should fear death or not?" and the answer is firm: "If our belief in Jesus is true, it is not proper that we fear death.... But if we don't believe in Jesus or give ourselves to Him, then we should indeed fear death, so our souls and spirits can be moved to reject our sins quickly and trust in Jesus, the Savior" (Methodist Overseas Mission Trust Association 1938: 268–269).[8]

Publics Defined by Death

In the early nineteenth century, Wesleyan authorities announced that "The circumstances of all remarkable deaths shall be drawn up at large, and sent to the Editor of our Magazine, who may publish them as far as he judges proper" (Warren 1827: 155). Accordingly, missionaries kept track of how people died, describing death scenes in their diaries and official reports; the Allen, Collocott, and Nolan examples cited earlier all came from annual reports for the Kadavu Division of the Methodist Church. The magazine *Wesleyan Missionary Notices* printed the accounts from Webb and White, also cited, and Polglase's letter was published in the *Occasional Paper[s]. . . of the Ladies' Committee for Ameliorating the Condition of Women in Heathen Countries, Female Education, &c.* Missionaries also described happy deaths in their published memoirs. For example, the autobiography of Joeli Bulu, a Tongan missionary who had a great impact on the development of the early church in Fiji, was translated and published by the Wesleyan Mission House in 1871. Describing his time on Ono-i-Lau Island in Fiji's far southeast, Bulu observed that "their dying words used to make my heart glow and burn within me," and then went into considerable detail about the deaths of two islanders, Daniela Kepa and Reuben (Bulu 1871: 49–54). The account of Reuben's death is particularly notable for the way it echoes accounts of Jesus's resurrection in the gospels, especially John 20:11–17.[9]

Such accounts of happy deaths helped create a Christian public of appreciative readers back home. Bright and cheerful deathbeds—Reuben announced that he saw Jesus and angels there in the room with him—were presented as stories of success, and the emotionally charged scenes were likely to raise funds for future work. Some authors, however, expressed a pseudo-Darwinian certainty that other "races" were doomed to extinction, placing missionaries metaphorically at the deathbeds of entire societies. In a journal entry from 1867, the Methodist missionary and amateur anthropologist Lorimer Fison stated that Fijians "can be made fit for Heaven: but they cannot be made fit for Earth. . . . I feel assured that they must perish from off ye face of ye earth" (Gunson 1994: 304–305). In 1905, the Anglican Bishop of Melanesia foresaw an imminent end to Melanesians as a people and wrote, "We are placed then by GOD in His infirmary, to work amongst a dying race; but a race which will certainly die a Christian death" (Wilson 1905: 7).

At first glance, it seems that one of the most remarkable things about these deaths is the distance from their audience in terms of geographical space: these good Christians were passing away on tropical islands that most readers would never see. Perhaps more remarkable was that these accounts, by resonating with previous accounts—whether historical, as in the case of Ratu Cakobau and the Reverend Hunt, or biblical, as in the case of Reuben and Jesus—helped to build a Christian public over time as well as space. Deathbed performances became public events by becoming texts that articulated with other texts. As Warner puts it, "It's the way texts circulate, and become the basis for further representations, that convinces us that publics have activity and duration. A text, to have a public, must continue to circulate through time, and because this can only be confirmed through an intertextual environment of citation and implication, all publics are intertextual, even intergeneric" (2002: 97).

As described, both public/private and life/death are fractally recursive contrasts, the terms standing in a mutually constitutive relationship that can be recalibrated at different levels of comparison. Here, I am attempting to bring these two halves together—public and private, and life and death—in their creative and consequential deployment in social life. How is death a nexus around which public–private distinctions are made?

Circulating texts that define publics may refer explicitly to manners of death, as in missionaries' narratives of deathbed scenes. More generally, social groups may be defined by how they die. One particularly well-known example is Japanese warriors, both samurai ("As he has to die, the aim of a samurai should be to fall performing some great deed of valor that will astonish both friend and foe alike," Daidoji Yuzan 1988: 63) and *tok-kotai* ("kamikaze"), expected to fall like cherry blossoms for the emperor (Ohnuki-Tierney 2002). In the West, a phenomenon remarked on by writers such as George Orwell (2000 [1946]) and David Sudnow (1967) is that social classes tend to die differently, not simply in the manners of their deaths but also in their sites and significances.

Sudnow, in his analysis of death announcements at US hospitals, shows how public and private are fractally recursive contrasts shaped by practices of managing discourse circulation. (Writing in 1967, he did not use this terminology.) He describes US hospitals as public places in which death is consciously managed as a private event. These publicly located deaths are made into private affairs through such strategies as spatial organization (such as assigning very sick patients to separate rooms, or drawing curtains around the bed if they have died in a communal room) and speech requirements (for example, not referring directly to death, and not announcing death in front of nonfamily members). In taking relatives to a separate room and assuming an air of concern and sympathy, the doctor creates a private space within the hospital's public space; to announce the death within the public zone where other patients and nonrelatives could hear it would be considered undignified and offensive.

As missionaries entextualized Fijian deaths, they were also attempting to erase local narratives of journeys to the afterworld of Burotu. In creating a Christian reading public, they ultimately tried to exclude competing narratives. Their efforts, however, moved "demons" into a new private space, especially for deaths that are not happy, as I now describe for a case from 2003.

Publicity, Privacy, and Demons

The pre-Christian Fijian afterlife was extensively narrativized, and dying subjects prepared carefully for their journey when they had the chance, as described earlier. Their success on the journey to Burotu depended not only on their encounters with fantastic creatures—the ferryman, fisher-fiends, and goddesses with gnashing teeth—but also on their actions while they were alive. The ways one might have displeased the gods during life included not getting tattooed (for women) and not killing anyone (for men). A monster named Naqanaqa specifically targeted men who had died without marrying (Nayacakalou 1961; Williams 1982 [1858]: 244–245, 248).

With the arrival of Christianity, this complex of narratives was muted. A new voice rang out, the voice of the missionary at the deathbed, earnestly announcing another happy death as proof of Christianity's triumph in the islands, the replacement of Burotu with Jehovah's heaven. But while missionaries succeeded spectacularly in converting indigenous Fijians to Christianity, they did not completely succeed in reshaping local beliefs about the spirit world and the afterlife. In the present day, many Methodists believe that old, non-Christian spirits still exist and can curse the living. Postmortem rituals still treat the deceased person's soul as a lingering entity. And while modern Fijians believe in Christian heaven and hell, they can also identify a particular point on each island as the site where souls jump into the sea, a pre-Christian feature of the sacred landscape.

Missionaries introduced new characters such as Jesus (*Jisu*) and Jehovah (*Jiova*) to Fijian spiritual imaginations. They also lexically displaced ancestral spirits into the realm of "devils" and "demons" through the loanwords *tevoro* and *timoni*. A general term for spirits, *kalou*, was adopted for the Christian God and given the definite article *Na*, making "god" into "The God"; certain ancestral spirits are known as *kalou vu*, "original gods." The result of these lexical and conceptual shifts is that present-day Fijian Methodism recognizes the Christian Trinity (God the Father, Jesus the Son, and the Holy Spirit) but also reserves space for a wide range of ancestral spiritual figures as well as nonhuman spirits. In short, non-Christian spirits continue to exist, and they occasionally threaten people's well-being.

Untimely deaths are one kind of crisis that can prompt new stories of the demonic. A key point, however, is that these stories cannot always be told publicly. In fact, demonic narratives may be exactly the kind of narrative that people want to circulate but know they cannot, or must be extremely cautious about if they do so, using methods of indirection and channels of gossip.

In June 2003, a leading chief from Tavuki village in Kadavu passed away in middle age. People were distraught because he was a popular and influential leader, and his passing seemed much too soon. Several days after the funeral, I heard the village steward describe a dream in which he had seen the late chief. In the dream, which the man recounted to the Methodist minister and the catechist in my presence, the late chief was trying to "catch" him.[10] The steward thought that the chief wanted to tell him something, but said that four people took the chief away. He added that he had told the chief, "You're dead!"

A week later, I asked the steward if I might tape-record his dream narrative, thinking it would be acceptable because he had already told the story once in my presence. To my surprise, he immediately said "tabu rawa" (it's impossible) and looked distraught. Seeing that I had touched a nerve, I said that this was fine with me. I think my quick retreat surprised him, however, for as our conversation was concluding, he said that he would let me record the story when I was just about to leave Tavuki, and that I could listen to it in the United States. As I wrote in my fieldnotes of June 28, "He didn't want folks *here* to hear it."

Things became clearer, but also more complicated, the next day. I was told that the four figures in the steward's dream—the people who came to take the late chief away—were not ancestors but living people. This meant that his dream was not just a ghost story, but a story about sorcery. In other words, in his dream he had seen the people who were probably responsible for the chief's untimely death.[11]

This event was striking for its aspect of privacy: the steward had a story that he desperately wanted to tell but not tell publicly. He told the leading church authorities in Tavuki, and, because I was present and he presumably thought I would not gossip about his tale, I happened to hear it, too. But when I proposed recording the story, he was quite upset at the thought that it might gain a public audience within Fiji. As I interpret the situation, his intentions were not at issue, but he apparently knew his story functioned as an accusation. The untimely death of a good Christian and respected chief had spun into a new kind of narrative: one that could not be told in a Fijian public space.[12]

These events occurred after the chief had passed away, not on his deathbed. In fact, the chief had died at a hospital in Suva, and his body was brought home to Kadavu for burial. But Fijian funerary practices mark a number of days after the burial as ones of special ritual observance: the fourth and one hundredth "nights after" are particularly significant, and the tenth-night increments (e.g., tenth, twentieth, etc., up until the hundredth) can also be observed, generally with copious kava drinking, ceremonial exchange, and the observance of taboos. Other death rituals may take place later yet (Arno 2003). In other words, ritual attention is paid to the spirit of the not fully departed person: "Only after the ceremonies for the hundredth night [after burial] can one be sure the dead will rest—especially those whose death was untimely or who were installed chiefs" (Toren 2004: 233; see also Herr 1981). In this context, it is not surprising that the steward had his dream, a manifestation of anxiety and perhaps a latent accusation, during this period shortly after the chief's death.

Indeed, he was not the only one with a tale to tell. A middle-aged woman from Tavuki village told me another story, which I did record on tape, of a young man from Suva who had come to Kadavu for the chief's funeral. The young man reportedly had the gift of "vision" from the Holy Spirit, enabling him to see the true nature of things. One night he saw a demon.

On that night, he had asked a woman whom I will call "Bulou Ana" to go with him to the edge of the village (*Bulou* is a Kadavu title for a chiefly woman). Then a woman named Esita from a nearby village came and said that she wanted to go home, and the young man from Suva agreed that he and the Bulou would accompany her on the path (Text 4.1). (In this story, all of the people's names have been changed because of the sensitive nature of the events.)[13]

When the narrator finished, I asked for confirmation of the final detail, saying "Tautauvata" (meaning "The same"), and she agreed, explaining, "Right. He had changed into a cat" (Io. O kia sa visautakini kia me je pusi). Then she provided a fuller description of demons, and how their hidden nature can be revealed (Text 4.2).

Bulou Ana had seen a *demon* or *devil*—the terms are used almost interchangeably—twice without realizing it. Once, the demon had appeared as a tall man; the other time it had appeared as a beautiful cat. Only the young visitor from Suva recognized this evil being for what it really was. The story blends the pre-Christian belief that spirits can appear as animals, which are called their "vessels" (*waqawaqa*), with the Christian belief that the Holy Spirit can give spiritual vision to humans. The most intriguing aspect of the story is not its syncretism, however, but the way it situates demons—like death—as disrupters of boundaries. They are entirely visible yet deceptively so: everyone could see the beautiful white cat, but only the young man with the vision could see its true identity. This inverts the case of people seeing angels on their deathbeds, with agency shifted here to the blessed among the living. In each case, the central figure can see the truth behind appearances.

The story does not present demons as private beings, but hidden ones. The privacy of the demonic sphere became evident, however, in the story's own disruptive afterlife when I gave the cassette tape to a friend who was going to transcribe it. He did so, but he chose to do his work at a kava-drinking session, where other drinkers overheard the woman's tale and became upset. I was mortified at this turn of events, rightly blaming myself for not ensuring that the story would remain private. I knew I had committed a serious, potentially consequential error; it could make the narrator a target of accusations. The more I fretted over the situation, however, the more puzzled I became. Why had my friend chosen to play the tape where others would hear it? Was there a specific reason that he wanted this particular demonic narrative to gain public circulation?

Text 4.1

Ia kacei sa via rauta jiko beka na tolu na kaloko se na va na kaloko i na bogibogi lailai ka. Sa mani drutu vimuri sara, drutu lai cava i Naituvasolo, kedratou ko Seru drutu sa lako jiko mai.... Ia drutu sa lako jiko mai ko Seru, i dua talega na turaga balavu, ulu levu, i bera jiko mai vei kedratou ko Seru. Ia o Bulou Ana mani vayadratakini kedratou sara, turaga talega ka drutu lako vata jiko mai.

And it was like three o'clock or four o'clock in the morning then. They followed along, they reached Naituvasolo, they [and another man named] Seru came.... Seru and they were coming, another tall man, with a big Afro hairstyle, was behind them. And Bulou Ana said good morning to them, to the man who was also coming along.

Ia na gauna drutu sa tasivi mai ke, o ere na turaga kia ka dru lako vata jiko i Bulou Ana, sa kaia sara vei Bulou Ana, "A, Naita, kedaru me daru sa lesu tale i Tavuki." Sa mani tukuni vei Esita, sa mani tukuna o Esita, "O, sa vinaka muru lesu tale, au sa lako i Natumua." Kedruka sa mani tuvuki lesu tale mai Naituvasolo dru lesu tale mai Tavuki, ia kedratou ko Seru drutu sa mada sara mai....

And when they were cutting across there, the man who came with Bulou Ana [the young man from Suva] said to Bulou Ana, "Ah, Naita [a relationship term], we should go back to Tavuki." Then he said it to Esita, and Esita said, "Oh, it's fine for you two to return, I'm going to Natumua." Then they turned around at Naituvasolo, they were returning to Tavuki, they [and] Seru were leading the way....

Kedruka dru lako mai cei, sa dana sara o Bulou Ana i dua na pusi rairaivinaka ni jiko i salevu. O kia sa qai vinakata, i domona nona roka, i vulavula vinaka qai vani damudamu tu valailai vanikacei. Damudamu tu valailai.... Kia sa qai vinakata, sa qai domona na pusi. Vinakata sara ga me je nona. Kia sa qai lakova jiko na kaciva jiko na pusi me lako mai vua. Ia na cauravou ka bera jiko mai ka, kia sa qai kidava ni dua tani na ere, ni o kia i dau vision. Sa qai dana o kia sa qai tukuna vanika vei Bulou Ana, "Naita, o, o ni rawa ni cici?"

They were going there, [and] Bulou Ana saw a beautiful cat on the path. And she wanted to have it, she loved its color, it was a nice white with a tinge of red there. A little bit of red.... And she wanted it, loved that cat. She wanted it to be hers. And she went to call the cat to come to her. But the young guy who was behind her there, he was surprised by something else, because he had the vision. And he saw it, and he went like this to Bulou Ana, "Naita...can you run?"

Sa vani sara ka o Bulou Ana, "Baleta?"

Bulou Ana was like, "Why?"

"Sega. Kevaka o ni rawa ni cici, o yau me'u vakasava na pusi."

"It's nothing. If you can run, I'm going to chase the cat away."

Kaia sara o Bulou Ana, "Na yava i jila?".. .

Bulou Ana said, "What did it do?".. .

Kaia sara... o Naita, na turaga cauravou ka, "Na, na pusi ka, na pusi ya, koya na turaga datou a sota mai, mai, mai mua ni wavu. O iko kila na turaga balavu kia ka dou vei—muru ma vivayadrataki?"

[Her] Naita, the young guy, said, "The, this cat, that cat, it's the man we met at, at, at the edge of the bridge. Did you know the tall man that we—you said good morning to?"

"Mino, au mino ni kilai kia.".. .

"No, I didn't know him.".. .

"Na turaga balavu sara ga kacei na pusi kari."

"That tall man is this cat."

Text 4.2

Na jimoni, i levu vei kedra i rawa ni visautakini kia me je pusi, rawa ni visautakini kia me je koli, rawa ni visautakini kia me je kuve, rawa ni dua ga na manumanu. Keda da i lako yatu, da dana, i rawa ni visautakini kia me dua na manumanu vuka, keda da i na mino ni kila. Kia ga i jiko vua na isolisoli ni Yalo Tabu, na vision, i rawa ni dana. Keda ka da i lako tu, da i lako tu ga da i mino ni kila. Keda sa dana ga, "O, na pusi." O Bulou Ana kacei kodriva baleta nona domona nona roka i taleitakina qai vinakata sara ga me kauta. O kia na turaga ka i jiko vua na isolisoli kacei, o kia qai dana ni dua tani. Ni mini je pusi ka dina. Ka na tevoro.

A lot of demons can change themselves into cats, can change themselves into dogs, can change themselves into rats, into an animal. We go out, we see, [a demon] can change into a bird, [but] we won't know it. Only those who have the gift of the Holy Spirit, the vision, can see. We people going about, we people going about, we don't know it. We just see it, "Oh, a cat." Bulou Ana ran there because of her love of that color [the cat's beautiful whiteness], she loved it, and really wanted to get it [the cat]. The man who had that gift [of vision], he saw that it was something else. That it wasn't really a cat. It was a devil.

I could only guess at the answers—asking him directly would have been too confrontational, no matter how politely I worded my questions—but my guesses puzzled and unsettled me further. The best answer I could come up with was that he heard the story as a covert accusation that his clan was responsible for the chief's death, as indicated by one of several signs: the cat as vessel (because different kin groups' origin gods take different animal forms) or the place that the demon was seen, for example. By playing the tape in public, perhaps he wanted everyone to know that he was aware of others' suspicions about his kin group. The story's publicization might serve as my friend's refutation of any accusations.

Thankfully, the controversy passed relatively quickly. To my knowledge, the narrator did not suffer any repercussions from the story. I was left with a lingering sense of embarrassment at my carelessness. In terms of ethnographic understanding, the event pushed me to think further about something I had observed but not fully appreciated: the general suspicion cast on individuals acting alone. For example, sometimes when I had told people that I was going to visit another village, they would ask who would accompany me. Previously, I had seen this in a positive light, an inquiry into companionship; afterward, I could see the negative background to the question, the assumption that people walking alone on paths might be trying to avoid public scrutiny.[14]

It is no accident that these dangerous figures—sorcery suspects in one man's dream, a shape-shifting demon in one woman's story of a man with spiritual vision—emerged at the time they did, after the death of a high chief. The chief was a popular and respected leader known for his strong friendship with the previous superintendent minister of the Methodist Church, but his passing was not a happy death by most criteria: he died away from home, in a hospital, too young. In pre-Christian days, his wives would have been strangled to accompany him on his journey toward Burotu, for, just as the living should not wander on paths alone, so the dead should not be alone on their perilous journeys. The arrival of the missionaries introduced a new story about the afterlife, one with a foreshortened narrative arc: the deathbed itself became the scene worth replaying, and the end of the story was a unification of the deceased person with Jesus in heaven. In reporting happy deaths, missionaries helped to form Christian publics who could participate in these generic moments of salvation. This focus on markedly Christian deathbeds, coupled with the classification of ancestral spirits as demons and devils, helped create a new, private, demonic realm. This realm is defined partly by signs that cannot or should not circulate publicly, like dreams of malicious killers and gossip about cats on dark night paths, as the novel articulations begun in the nineteenth century are still being worked out in the spiritual imaginations of the twenty-first.

5

A *Chorus of Assent Will Lift Us All*

*In all areas of life and ideological activity, our speech is
filled to overflowing with other people's words.*
BAKHTIN, Discourse in the Novel

At some stage we'll need to shut some people up.
COUP LEADER AND PRIME MINISTER VOREQE
BAINIMARAMA[1]

BAKHTIN'S OBSERVATION THAT "the word in language is half someone
else's" (1981: 293) has become widely accepted among scholars. A "dialogic orientation," as Bakhtin put it, "is the natural orientation of any living discourse" (279), meaning that no speaker is the sole author of his or
her utterances. One always speaks in dialogue with past utterances and
expected future responses, and the establishment of distinct "voices" in
discourse is an ongoing, interactive project. The model of dialogism has
given fresh critical perspectives to scholars analyzing the systematics of
power (e.g., Kaplan and Kelly 1994) and added depth and resonance to
ethnographic writing by encouraging nuanced complexity rather than
artificial unity, notes of dissonance disrupting orchestrated harmony.

Yet discussions of dialogism occasionally miss the fact that some speakers do present their words as pure truths from single sources transcend-
ing all contexts. That is, some speakers deny that the word is half someone
else's, insisting instead that they represent the singular voice of God or the
people, for example. In Bakhtin's terms, such speakers attempt to harness
discourse's "centripetal force," its "unifying, centralizing" tendencies that
counterpose its "centrifugal force" of stratification and decentralization
(Bakhtin 1981: 272–273).

Since his coup of December 2006, Fiji's military commander and self-selected prime minister, Commodore Voreqe ("Frank") Bainimarama, has consistently attempted to generate centripetal force in his discourse in order to facilitate his rule. He and his associates, like many others in autocratic regimes, seem to believe that if everyone in the nation says the same thing, they will all think with one mind and move with one accord. Rather than a one-track mind, Bainimarama seeks a one-mind track: a path with no dissent. In this imaginary world, unity of expression will give the nation the momentum it needs to escape, at last, its beleaguered past of ethnic and religious strife.

In this chapter, I explore the actions of Bainimarama and his associates by drawing on a model of *monologue* derived from Bakhtin. As mentioned in Chapter 1, Bakhtin described monologic projects during the Enlightenment in which unity was "illustrated through the image of a single consciousness: the spirit of a nation, the spirit of a people, the spirit of history, and so forth. Everything capable of meaning can be gathered together in one consciousness and subordinated to a unified accent" (1984: 82). Note that, for Bakhtin, pure monologue is impossible: discourse is always dialogic. Yet centripetal forces can be pushed to extremes, as I observed in the brief discussion of the sayings of Chairman Mao in Chapter 1. When I use the term "monologue," then, I am not suggesting that an autocratic leader such as Bainimarama really composes his utterances (or has them composed for him) in a context-free, discursive vacuum, but rather that when he speaks he portrays his words as those of a unified will which, because already unified, cannot receive a meaningful response. As Bruce Mannheim and Dennis Tedlock write, monologue is a form of expression for which one "expects no answer" (1995: 1–2).

Before proceeding, I must offer four brief caveats. First, for simplicity's sake, I will describe Bainimarama as the author of various statements and documents, but he is more accurately called the "animator"—that is, the one who pronounces the words or, as Goffman memorably puts it, "the sounding box in use... the talking machine" (Goffman 1981: 144). Someone else might well be formulating the ideas and drawing up the plans that Bainimarama, as head of government, issues. (An aristocrat and lieutenant colonel in the Fijian army, Ratu Tevita Mara, who fled Fiji in 2011 when he became aware of a plan to arrest him, declared that Bainimarama was "morally and intellectually bankrupt, [and]... no more than [Attorney General] Aiyaz Khaiyum's hand puppet" (Mara 2011).) The second caveat is that monologic projects are not necessarily successful.

A monologic speaker may well expect no answer, but this does not mean that listeners will not attempt to turn the monologue into a dialogue, in which speakers' words echo with and recontextualize each other. Indeed, the Bainimarama government's monological project cannot be deemed successful by most measures, as I demonstrate below. The third caveat is that I focus only on the period between 2006 and 2011. Thus, while I discuss the abrogation of Fiji's constitution in April 2009, I do not cover the events of 2012 and 2013, when Bainimarama rejected a new constitution (which had been drafted by an independent commission) and had his attorney general's office draw up a new one. Even though I do not discuss more recent events, they have displayed the monological tendencies described in this chapter. Finally, although monologues may be characteristic of autocratic regimes, I do not take the moral stance that dialogue is inherently good and monologue inherently bad. In some contexts, such as Indo-Fijian *pancayat* as described by Donald Brenneis (1990), monologue can be framed as a consensual project, with participants hoping to create a single, definitive public account of an event that is meant to ensure disputing parties' good reputations. Conversely, "dialogue can be tyrannical" (Peters 1999: 34; see also Urban and Smith 1998), especially to the degree that it is fetishized and treated as a cure for every conceivable problem.

Shutting Up, Shutting Down

After Fiji gained its independence from Great Britain in 1970, the new nation endured three coups in its first three decades. Lieutenant Colonel Sitiveni Rabuka executed two coups in 1987, and a civilian, George Speight, led one in 2000. Their acts were carried out in the name of indigenous rights, with Indo-Fijians (citizens of Indian descent) demonized as greedy foreigners seeking too much political influence. During the coups, leaders of the politically influential Methodist Church tended to support the rebellion in the name of indigenous rights and against perceived Indo-Fijian economic and political power. Rabuka, himself a Methodist, stated that his coup was a mission from God, and his supporters rallied to unite fundamentalist Christianity with indigenous Fijian identity. In doing so, they expressed several themes that are firm doctrine for Fijian ethnonationalists: the belief that chiefs' power comes from God, the assertion that tradition is morally superior to modernity, and the certainty that indigenous sovereignty and land ownership are perpetually threatened and must be defended.

In the coup of 2000, Speight did not invoke Christian identity the way Rabuka had done, but some of his supporters repeated popular Christian themes. One evangelical leader reasoned that just as Rabuka had been a Moses for indigenous Fijians, so Speight was their Joshua (Ratuva 2002: 21). Both, that is, were biblical types called by God to champion the indigenous Christian cause against the "heathen" (Hindu and Muslim) Indo-Fijians. Speight did try to imitate Rabuka in various ways, especially by portraying himself as a defender of indigenous interests. But the differences between the two coup leaders were stark, and they came to very different ends. Rabuka prospered, becoming prime minister in 1992, and then, after losing that position in the election of 1999, chairman of the prestigious Great Council of Chiefs. Speight was convicted of treason and remains in prison to this day.

Two of the most significant differences between the coups of 1987 and 2000 were the military's role and the degree of violence that erupted. Rabuka's actions, supported by the military, unleashed violence and acts of intimidation, especially against Indo-Fijians, but no one was killed in the turmoil. In contrast, "at least 20 people died violently as a direct result of Speight's folly" (Field, Baba, and Nabobo-Baba 2005: 261; see also Trnka 2008: 46–47). While not all soldiers supported Speight's coup, a key faction did: elite troops from the Counter Revolutionary Warfare Unit (CRWU), who took hostages at parliament, ultimately holding some of them for eight weeks (Ratuva 2007: 30). Bainimarama, who was the military commander at the time, eventually gained control of the situation by declaring martial law, appointing the civilian Laisenia Qarase as prime minister, and having Speight arrested.

Several months later, on November 2, 2000, members of the CRWU rebelled and attempted to kill Bainimarama as part of a plan to free jailed coup leaders, including Speight. Five of these mutineers were "tortured to death...[with] fractured eye sockets, bruising of the tongue, abrasion around the neck...dislocation of collar bones, bruising in the heart, collapsed lungs, bruising to the back of the knees" (Field, Baba, and Nabobo-Baba 2005: 244). Bainimarama, who barely escaped the attempt to kill him, denounced the military rebellion as "an attempt by Satan to destroy us" (245).

Qarase, the caretaker prime minister, led his party to electoral victory in 2001, and it seemed as though Fiji might return to normalcy—or at least recuperate to some extent—as it had done after Rabuka's coups. Over the next few years, however, Qarase antagonized Bainimarama by showing sympathy to indigenous ethnonationalists, and in response Bainimarama showed increasing hostility to the government. In October 2004, when the government sponsored events to promote national reconciliation under the banner of "Fiji Week," the armed forces "refused to take part in the ceremonies, saying that the apologies were meaningless without justice taking its course" (Ratuva 2007: 36). The military's distrust of the government intensified in 2005 when Qarase championed a piece of legislation called the Promotion of Reconciliation, Tolerance and Unity Bill. It offered amnesty to participants in Speight's coup, and Bainimarama saw it as a gift to those who had caused Fiji so much trouble and had almost killed him. As a result, Bainimarama offered sharper and sharper criticism of Qarase's government, going so far as to send military delegations to villages before the election of May 2006, urging people not to vote for Qarase's party (40–43).

Despite this ill will, Bainimarama insisted as early as April 2003 and as late as November 2006 that he would not execute a coup of his own.[2] After Qarase's party won the May election, however, it became evident that there would be a showdown—a kind of second resolution to the events of 2000. Fijian statesmen and foreign diplomats tried to reconcile the military and the government but failed, and in the month before the coup actually took place, "it was widely known in local diplomatic circles that there was going to be a military takeover, and that nothing short of utter capitulation, resignation by Qarase or installation of a puppet government could avert it" (Fraenkel 2007: 425). On December 5, Bainimarama overthrew the government. The next day, he "declared a state of emergency and promised stern repression against any who dared to incite popular resistance" (427).

Bainimarama's response to his critics since then has tended to employ four distinct but interconnected strategies. The first is redefinition, in which the coup is classified as not being a "coup" at all. Before the event had even taken place, Bainimarama described his actions as a "clean up," and as he reminisced to an Australian reporter almost four years later, "we didn't call it a coup, we called it a clean-up campaign."[3] Various speakers have echoed him, including the head of the Fiji Human Rights Commission, Shaista Shameem, and the prominent Catholic priest Kevin Barr, an anti-poverty activist who coauthored an opinion piece in the *Fiji Times* suggesting that this was not really a coup because "it was not a swift, sudden and unexpected event" and because "The commander was very reluctant to take over the reins of government."[4] Fiji's High Court, in a decision that legitimized Bainimarama's takeover and President Ratu Josefa Iloilo's support for it, decided in October 2008 that the president had simply "exercise[d] prerogative powers to rule directly" at a moment of crisis; as one legal scholar commented, "In effect, the Court held that there had been no coup" (Williams 2008: 4).

The second strategy Bainimarama has used to deal with his critics is exclusion. Potential agitators—most prominently, publishers and diplomats—are kicked out of the country. The publisher of the *Fiji Times* was deported in May 2008, and his successor was expelled in January 2009. In addition, the publisher of the *Fiji Sun* was sent home to Australia in February 2008. The government then announced in June 2010 that Fiji's media sources needed to have a local ownership stake of at least 90 percent; by this decision, it forced the sale of the *Fiji Times*, previously controlled by Rupert Murdoch's conglomerate.[5] The governments of Australia and New Zealand have had their high commissioners summarily deported, with Australia's diplomats ejected in November 2009 and July 2010, and New Zealand's receiving the same treatment in June 2007, December 2008, and November 2009.

Within the country, too, leaders have been shut up and shut down. During a round of "dialogue forums" in early 2009, in which the leaders of major political parties had been discussing Fiji's future, the leaders of four particular parties were told the day before the third forum that they were no longer welcome. One of them was Qarase's Soqosoqo Duavata ni Lewenivanua party (SDL), thrown out of government in Bainimarama's coup. Another was the National Federation Party (NFP), historically an Indo-Fijian stronghold and Fiji's oldest political party (Lal 2000b: 26). The third member of a coalition with the SDL and NFP, the United Generals Party (UGP), was also banned from the forum by Bainimarama. In short, Bainimarama excluded the dominant party associated with indigenous Fijian interests (Qarase's SDL), a strong if no longer dominant Indo-Fijian party (NFP), and the one representing non-Fijian and non-Indian interests (UGP). Qarase complained that Bainimarama's forum was simply "a collection of parties who failed to win seats in the last election or did not contest it because they lacked support."[6]

In addition, Bainimarama dismissed the Great Council of Chiefs (Bose Levu Vakaturaga), a colonially instituted advisory board that had appointed senators, the president, and vice president of independent Fiji.[7] Shortly before his coup, Bainimarama ridiculed the council by stating that if it could not make Qarase accept the military's ultimatums, "then they should meet under a mango tree and enjoy home brew"—an image of lazy old men with nothing to do but get drunk, and not even drunk on kava, at that.[8] Bainimarama's sneer became a snarl after his choice for a new vice president was rejected by the council in April 2007. The next day, Bainimarama called the council a "security threat in our efforts to move the country forward," suspended its activities, and announced that it "will only be reconvened if, and when, the interim government sees it appropriate" (Lal 2009: 79). He later abolished the council in March 2012.

The third strategy Bainimarama has used is legal intimidation, including the issuance of emergency decrees. Immediately after executing his coup, he declared a state of emergency which remained in force until May 31, 2007, at which point the government "cautioned the people that it would continue to deal with anyone who incites public instability and disorder" (Kotobalavu 2009: 376). Almost two years later, a new set of Public Emergency Regulations was published on the day the Constitution was abrogated (discussed later) and renewed until January 2012. Using the emergency regulations, issued under the authority of President Ratu Josefa Iloilo, Bainimarama cancelled the Methodist Church's planned annual conference for 2009 and later announced that the Methodists would not be allowed to hold any conferences until 2014 at the earliest, the year for which he had set Fiji's next election. He did this, he explained, because Methodist leaders were discussing political rather than spiritual matters. A total of twenty-seven Methodist Church officials were charged with violating the Public Emergency Regulations, more than half of them for holding a meeting of the church's standing committee (komiti ni leqa) in July 2009. Among those charged were the church's general secretary and president.[9]

Besides controlling the movement of people in this way, the emergency regulations also controlled the movement of information. Specifically, they targeted the news media:

> Where the Permanent Secretary for Information has reason to believe that any broadcast or publication may give rise to disorder and may thereby cause undue demands to be made upon the police or the Armed Forces, or may result in a breach of the peace, or promote disaffection or public alarm, or undermine the Government and the State of Fiji, he or she may, by order, prohibit such broadcast or publication. (Fiji Government 2009: 15)

The broad scope of this decree resulted in general censorship of Fiji's media outlets. Of Fiji's three daily newspapers, two had many of their stories suppressed by government censors, while the third, the *Fiji Sun*, evolved into a pro-government publication. Stories, both domestic and foreign, were forbidden if they were deemed to be negative in any way. For example, according to a journalist whose name I must keep confidential for obvious reasons, stories banned by government censors included one on lethal police brutality in Papua New Guinea, one on same-sex marriage in New Hampshire, one on increased unemployment in Australia, and a cartoon about Colin Powell. The journalist told me that the government got so wrapped up in the project of censorship that it once attempted to remove a story that it had submitted to the newspaper itself. "When we pointed out that [the Permanent Secretary for Information, Lieutenant Colonel Neumi] Leweni himself had sent it," he observed wryly, "they naturally relented."

When the emergency regulations of 2009 first came into effect, the *Fiji Times* briefly responded by calling attention to its censorship, leaving white space in place of deleted articles, with the explanation "This story could not be published due to Government restrictions" (Figure 5.1). Unamused, "Leweni warned them he would close their business if that continued."[10] The smallest of the dailies, the *Daily Post*, responded with more panache by replacing censored articles with news parodies. For example, an article in the *Post* with the headline "Man gets on bus" reported:

> In what is believed to be the first reported incident of its kind, a man got on a bus yesterday.
>
> "It was easy," he said.
>
> "I just lifted one leg up and then the other and I was on."
>
> *Fiji Daily Post* reporters found witnesses willing to confirm the happening.
>
> "Yes," said one who asked to remain anonymous, "I saw him get on the bus."...
>
> Students from a local school who had been waiting for two hours in the rain for the bus also confirmed that they saw the man board.
>
> "We are happy for him," one student remarked in terms reminiscent of Neil Armstrong (the first man to step onto the moon): "it may be one small step for him, but it is one giant step for the people of Fiji."

Another promise

President reassures nation on 2014 election

THE interim Government will hold democratic parliamentary elections in September 2014, says President Ratu Josefa Iloilo.

Addressing the nation at Government House yesterday morning, Ratu Iloilo said he was sure we would all work together and the soon-to-be appointed interim government would ensure a smooth transition.

"I am sure you will work together with me and the soon-to-be-appointed interim govern-

ment to ensure that this transition to a new legal order is not only smooth but will reap many benefits for us and future generations and resolve many of our long-outstanding and systematic problems."

He said the announcement of a new Cabinet and other institutional appointments would be made over the next few days.

Ratu Iloilo believes that five years is necessary for an interim government to put into place the

necessary reforms and processes leading to an election.

"You may recall that I spoke to you in early January 2007 after executive authority was returned to me after the events of December 5, 2006.

"I subsequently appointed an interim prime minister and his Cabinet and gave them the mandate to adhere to. That interim government has been in existence for more than two years now."

He said given the circumstances, the interim government had performed extremely well.

Ratu Iloilo said the interim Government had brought about reforms and created opportunities for new ideas.

"It has adhered to my mandate. It has had a positive impact on the lives of our people in particular the ordinary citizens of our country, including those in the rural areas," he said.

THE Citizens Constitutional Forum believes the re-appointment of the interim Government could have been accommodated within the Court of Appeal ruling, Forum executive director Reverend Akuila Yabaki said there was provision within the court ruling for the President of Fiji to appoint an independently interim government or otherwise. Mr Yabaki said the abrogation of the Constitution was not necessary and was unfortunate.

This story could not be published due to Government restrictions.

This story could not be published due to Government restrictions.

This story could not be published due to Government restrictions.

This story could not be published due to Government restrictions.

FIGURE 5.1 Part of page 3 in the *Fiji Times*, April 12, 2009.

Such parody news, with its winking use of journalistic cliché, ran alongside regular news; the juxtaposition of articles could be read as a commentary on the absurdity of censorship. Two days after the story appeared about the man getting on the bus, the *Post* ran a serious article on the lower left-hand corner of page 2 in which Leweni denied talk of a planned curfew and said, "We strongly encourage the public to go about their lives just as they were before the court case and the subsequent abrogation of the Constitution." On the upper right-hand corner of the same page, a satirical article titled "Man goes out" announced: "It's official: a man went out. Neighbours reported that they saw him go out last night.... Asked where he would go, the man said 'out.' "[11]

Finally, the fourth strategy is physical intimidation. Death threats have proliferated in Fiji since Bainimarama's coup. In August 2007, a trade union leader named Taniela Tabu who had been taken to the military barracks—apparently because of a statement he had made that was critical of Bainimarama—reported that "I was warned that next time I am taken up (to the camp [the Queen Elizabeth Barracks]) I will be killed." He added that two other prominent union leaders, Attar Singh and Tevita Koroi, had been threatened with death, too, saying "The threat to kill me, Attar Singh and Tevita Koroi is real.... I want the world to know that."[12] Later that month, deposed prime minister Qarase reported that he had received a telephone call in which "The caller said the military was happy I was returning to Suva on Friday but they would be waiting for me and take me once I touched down at Nausori airport and kill me."[13]

In May 2008, Australia's high commissioner in Suva received a series of written death threats that were prominently reported in the newspapers, although the text of the threats has not been made publicly available. Besides these spoken and written threats, some critics of the military government, including the editor of the *Fiji Times*, have had their cars vandalized and their houses attacked with petrol bombs. When the eminent Indo-Fijian historian Brij Lal criticized the deportation of one of the Australian high commissioners, he was taken to the military barracks in Suva, roughed up, spat upon, verbally abused, and "told to leave the country within twenty four hours or face the consequences. I was left in no doubt what those consequences would be: my family might have to fetch my body from the morgue if I did not obey orders" (Lal 2011: 304). Finally, in 2011, WikiLeaks revealed that the US embassy in Suva had reported that Bainimarama personally assaulted a civil servant in 2006, telling him, "Don't fuck with the military."[14]

In early February 2009, a Methodist Church official handed me a photocopy of a printout of recent blog postings, one of which read in part: "The Methodist Church is a sham. Its leaders (who spend time abusing young children) drive around in expensive vehicles while its members scrounge [a]round for morsels of food.... People such as [Church president] Tuikilakila Waqairatu should be strung by their feet and the people of this country should stone these heathens to death for their comments and actions which have led this country to the brink of a racial war" (IG-Fiji 2009). This is a public assertion of lethal desire rather than a specific death threat. But in the context of the other threats, it gains a kind of generic force as another attempt to silence dissent. For, while the people making these phone calls, sending these letters, and posting on these blogs are not officially known, their targets are all people who have taken stances opposing the military-led government. In Goffman's terms, Bainimarama's government was unquestionably the "principal" behind these threats: "someone whose position is established by the words that are spoken, someone whose beliefs have been told, someone who is committed to what the words say" (Goffman 1981: 144). Since December 2006, what these words have been saying is this: speak from the same script that we do, or else stay silent.

Monologue

Monologue is not simply censorship. It is a paradoxically creative kind
of erasure, with erasure defined as "forms of forgetting, denying, ignor-
ing, or forcibly eliminating those distinctions or social facts that fail to fit
the picture of the world presented by an ideology" (Gal 2005: 27). In the
destructive creativity of monologue, one set of signs or texts is meant to
substitute for others, replacing them and precluding their future circulation. In being designed to replace other signs and texts, monologues betray
their dialogical origins; but in attempting to preclude the future circulation of those other signs and texts, and forbidding meaningful response,
monologues achieve their fullest form. This chapter's epigraph, in which
Bainimarama tells an Australian journalist that "at some stage we'll need
to shut some people up," is part of a longer explanation in which he makes
it clear that while some people need to be silenced, those who agree with
him need to speak up:

PHILIPPA MCDONALD: What about bringing back Radio Australia to Fiji?
BAINIMARAMA: What?
MCDONALD: Radio Australia?
BAINIMARAMA: What? So they can continue with this harping of what
  we're trying to do with regards to changes? A lot of people don't seem
  to understand, you know, PINA (Pacific Islands News Association),
  for once PINA, they came... they understood what we're trying to do
  here. They're saying that we're... and this is not an ordinary government, we're trying to bring about reforms and changes, and for that
  they understood that at some stage we'll need to shut some people
  up, and stop this from bringing about instability and stop that. They
  understand that. I don't see why [New Zealand prime minister] John
  Keys [sic] and your government can't understand that?[15]

In short, Bainimarama insists that he cannot speak unless dissenting others do not speak, and approves of those who say what he is saying. This
position is not a surprising one for an autocratic government to take, and
it suggests why foreign governments' attempts to engage in dialogues
with Bainimarama are likely to fail.

Such an understanding of effective language is characteristic of some
kinds of military discourse. Brij Lal quotes Fiji's first coup leader, Rabuka,
telling an audience in Canberra, "I was taught to command, not to lead,"

and Lal adds: "And that is absolutely right. The rules and rituals of politics, how that game was played, the massaging of egos, the cultivation of coalitions not through coercion but through consensus, was alien to military life" (Lal 2000a: 321). The ideology underlying this style of linguistic coercion might be called one of "command-and-compliance," in which the purpose of language is to effect unitary action, a lock-step response that does not and should not respond to the original utterance in any way other than to do as it says.[16] Matters of a speaker's intention are therefore beside the point; matters of effective response are what count. And because of this, requests for explanations of motive can provoke comically circular responses, as when a journalist asked Fiji's Permanent Secretary for Information Neumi Leweni about the sacking of the reserve bank's governor. "All I can say," Leweni replied, "is that this is what we have done."[17]

This understanding of language opens up new questions about Bakhtinian dialogism. Bakhtin argued that every meaningful utterance is a link in a chain of utterances, tied not only to previous ones but intended to articulate with future ones. Listening is an active process of planned response, and every speaker is situated as both listener and respondent to past and future utterances in the instant of expression. Bakhtin criticized the model of general linguistics in which a dyad of speaker-plus-hearer is the atom of communication; he wrote that "the listener who understands passively...does not correspond to the real participant in speech communication" (1986: 69). "However monological the utterance may be," he comments later in the same essay, "it cannot but be, in some measure, a response to what has already been said about the given topic, on the given issue....The utterance is filled with *dialogic overtones*" (1986: 92, emphasis in original). For Bakhtin, the only speaker who could theoretically be a monologuist was Adam, the first human, who did not need to orient himself to "the alien word" in any way (1981: 279).

This argument is well known, moving toward—if not already arrived at—the station of scholarly truism. And yet, a monological speaker attempts to place listeners precisely in that position of passive understanding that Bakhtin identified as a fiction of general linguistics. This passivity might be manifest in silence, but the goal of many speakers of political monologue is to generate a paradoxical kind of passive action in listeners: perfect transposition, in which the original utterance, its evaluative accent, and its intended effects are re-created by other speakers. The monologist says: do as I do *by* saying what I say.

Monologue is creative, then, but its creativity involves erasing competing discourse while presenting an alternative without compromise. Earlier,
I mentioned how Bainimarama has confronted the Methodist Church;
but he also briefly supported a competing denomination called the New
Methodists, led by the brother of the national police commissioner. (I discuss the New Methodists later.) I mentioned how Bainimarama's government used the Public Emergency Regulations to censor newspapers. It
does not only suppress, however; it rewrites. The journalist Sean Dorney
recounts how government censors turned a story about the European
Union's harsh criticism of "regressive developments in Fiji" into a sunny
proclamation of the EU's support for the country.[18] I mentioned the political dialogue forum, in which major party leaders were excluded. But the
key point is that minor party leaders were included and followed the
forum's rules for "dialogue," which, according to one wry commentator,
"read like a festival for the single-minded."[19] I mentioned the suspension
of the Great Council of Chiefs; this was followed by the government's con-
vening a meeting of minor chiefs, the Bose ni Turaga. A monologist does
not simply suppress others' speech, then, but urges others to speak in
particular ways, saying the "right" thing in a unified voice.

In speaking monologically, Bainimarama's government is engaging in
ritualized acts of entextualization that are meant to give legitimacy to a
government established by force. In these kinds of acts, as Kertzer (1988)
puts it, "rite makes might." Bainimarama's fullest attempt to speak monologically is seen in the case of the "Peoples Charter for Change, Peace
and Progress," a document written to map out Fiji's future, to which
I now turn.

Monologue in the "Peoples Charter"[20]

When he took power, Bainimarama insisted that he would eradicate the
racism, chiefly dominance, and religious bigotry that had fueled Fiji's previous political violence. A group called the National Council for Building
a Better Fiji (NCBBF) was formed for the task of composing the Peoples
Charter. The council's co-chairmen were Bainimarama and the Roman
Catholic archbishop of Suva, Petero Mataca, who had flagged his support
for the military shortly after the coup by writing in a *Fiji Times* opinion
piece: "I wish the new interim government well in its efforts and I call
upon all women and men of goodwill to assist in whatever way they can to
rebuild our beloved country."[21]

The Peoples Charter was incubated for more than a year. A preliminary document called "Building a Better Fiji for All through a People's Charter for Change & Progress" appeared in April 2007, although not until October that year was the council officially formed (NCBBF 2008b: i). The process of preparing the charter spawned other documents, including a "Report on the State of the Nation and the Economy" (NCBBF 2008c), which served as a reference point for the charter's criticisms of contemporary Fiji and its recommendations, and a "Consultation Document" which, according to the final version of the charter, was "widely distributed throughout the country" as the charter was being drafted (2008b: i). In August 2008, "over 250,000 copies of the Peoples Charter documents were published, in English and the vernacular [i.e., Standard Fijian and Fiji Hindi], and disseminated, as widely as possible, across the country" (2008b: iii). The final version was presented on December 15, 2008; it did not differ substantially from the August 2008 draft. Both decry Fiji's slide into mayhem and insist on a securely multiethnic future.[22]

After its foreword, the charter begins with eight pages of affirmations couched as what "we" believe, affirm, and do. The first page proclaims:

> We, the People of Fiji:
> - Awake, and We Arise
> - To a New Dawn
> - To a New Day, and a New Way
> - In Our Lives, as One Nation, as One People
> For We Are
> THE PEOPLE OF FIJI (NCBBF 2008b: 1)

The rest of the document follows this style, firing off aspirations in bullet points. Over the following forty pages, it attempts to do two separate things. First, it tries to inspire readers, to make them feel that the future is brighter than the present—to have faith that Fiji will prosper. Second, it tries to set a practical course, proposing specific actions that will transform the nation. The two goals can be combined, of course, but the combination is not a smooth one in the Peoples Charter. Indeed, it reads like a recipe for liberty shoved into the meat grinder of corporate prose. A reader might, perhaps, be stirred by the call to "arise to a new dawn" but would be knocked down again by the recommendation to "Accelerate the right-sizing of the public sector" and introduce "e-governance" (2008b: 24).[23]

Many of the statements in the document are vague, and their shared vagueness does not make a fruitful mixture.

The charter has several short introductory and concluding sections.[24] Between them stands the text's centerpiece, eleven "pillars" whose explanation and discussion spans pages nine to thirty-eight.[25] The presentation is the same for each: the pillar's title is followed by a discussion or list of "Critical Problems and Issues," followed in turn by recommendations for "The Way Forward." In this way, the document continually pivots between negative and positive, describing a problem afflicting Fiji and then explaining how it can be solved. The pillars mark topics that vary greatly in content and scope. Some are immediate practical concerns, such as improving Fiji's international relations. Others involve ambitious projects of social engineering, such as creating a single national identity and developing a democracy that will prevent future coups. Some are realistic, such as improving health care; others are less so, especially the plan to eliminate most poverty within seven years. Finally, some echo the global concerns of nongovernmental organizations, such as the call for better leadership, whereas others address issues that are especially pernicious in Fiji, such as the inequitable distribution of land.

In attempting to generate a textually coherent "we, the people of Fiji," the Peoples Charter refers to an oppositional force that it needs to overcome: "coup culture." This phrase has circulated widely inside and outside of Fiji, coming from both supporters and detractors of Bainimarama. The leader of Fiji's first coups, Sitiveni Rabuka, apologized for his actions two decades later, explaining, "Staging a coup is something no one should be proud of because you don't become a hero, so all the copycats should not think they will be heroes.... Let's put all that behind us and stop this coup culture because it does not help with development and progress."[26] But Bainimarama, one of Rabuka's "copycats," also used the phrase. In a speech to the United Nations General Assembly, he declared, "In response to this criticism [of his own coup] I say this. Fiji has a coup culture—a history of civilian or military coups executed in the interests of a few and based on nationalism, racism and greed."[27] Helen Clark, New Zealand's prime minister, stated in 2007 that "Fiji's development has been severely impeded by its manifest coup culture," and in 2009 Australia's prime minister Kevin Rudd—himself soon to be summarily deposed—picked up the phrase when he said, "We want to see stability in the South Pacific and we're not about to simply allow a coup culture to spread."[28]

The Peoples Charter uses the phrase "coup culture" three times. In the first pillar's discussion section, Fiji's voting system is criticized for including seats in Parliament for members of particular ethnic groups voted for by members of those groups. "The current communal system of representation entrenches inequalities," the authors argue, "by not providing one value for one vote, [and] has contributed to the 'coup culture', and the consequent ethnic-based politics that has impeded our national development" (NCBBF 2008b: 11). Two paragraphs later, the phrase returns: "In the wake of the coups since 1987, Fiji suffers the stigma of having a 'coup culture'. We must put an end to the cycle of coups" (2008b: 12). This sense of stigmatization—of the outside world's harsh judgment on Fiji for its routine chaos—returns in the discussion of pillar number eleven, where the authors write, "Fiji's image internationally is that it is a country prone to a 'coup culture', lawlessness and bad governance" (2008b: 38). The phrase is always placed in quotes which seem to stamp it as imported goods, but it is also presented matter-of-factly.[29] As a cliché, it circulates easily, fitting well into a monological project such as the Peoples Charter because it is already being pronounced by people on both sides of the issue. No one disputes that Fiji has a coup culture; they differ only in seeing Bainimarama's coup as cancer or cure.

A primary goal of political monologue is the creation of apparent cohesion, as seen in the case of the Peoples Charter and more successful projects like Chairman Mao's quotations. In this regard, the charter's second pillar begins by stating plainly: "We lack a common national identity and unity as citizens of Fiji" (NCBBF 2008b: 17). The authors offer a linguistic solution to this dilemma, proposing that all citizens be called "Fijian" but reserving the name "i-Taukei," literally meaning "owners," for indigenous Fijians (2008b: 18). The move to call all citizens "Fijian" might sound innocuous, but it is a controversial step. In December 2003, Senator Adi Litia Cakobau complained that Indo-Fijian scholars "call their study of fellow Indians 'Fijian studies.' This form of ethnic violence is extremely powerful," she asserted, "because like the AIDS virus, it is not visible or obvious to its victims....The Indians are writing the Fijian people out of existence right before our eyes and lack of awareness of their acts of ethnocide makes them extremely powerful."[30] The logic of her claim, put bluntly, is that the nation is the "race," and the term "Fijian" should be reserved exclusively for indigenous citizens. The Peoples Charter attempts to overcome such racism in the name of a nation purified by its heterogeneity, a multiethnic, multicultural, multifaith polity that agrees on everything due to the strong and central role of the military.

Before the Peoples Charter was formally accepted by the president in December 2008, the government tried to gain support for it by sending promotional teams to villages. This was an effort to create what Sally Falk Moore has called "ratifying bodies public," audiences whose presence seemingly grants legitimacy to a government's projects (Moore 1977). The promotional teams' methods, however, were reportedly coercive or duplicitous, or both. I spoke with one public servant who had worked for years in a rural district, and he recalled that when the government team came to his area they announced that if people did not support the charter, they would not receive assistance from the government. Indeed, this man told me, plans for building and staffing a local health clinic were cancelled when the district that would have hosted it came out against the charter. In 2009, I personally saw a map in a district commissioner's office that had red, green, and yellow pins stuck into it, indicating places that had respectively supported, opposed, and wavered on the charter. Another man, a civil servant based in Vitilevu, told me that government employees had been required to attend a study session regarding the charter the previous year. Afterward, they had been told to sign their names. Their signatures were then used as "proof" that they supported the charter. Reinforcing this sense that much support for the charter was either unwilling or unwitting, Fiji's national TV news program ran a story on November 16, 2008, in which a seventeen-year-old boy claimed that a policeman had approached him and his friends to sign the "response form" in support of the charter without telling them what it was (Fiji One National News 2008). At one point, the government claimed that more than 92 percent of all respondents supported the charter, a statistic that economist Wadan Narsey at the University of the South Pacific described as "just so much garbage."[31]

The Peoples Charter had one prominent opponent from the beginning: the Methodist Church, which had supported the coups of 1987 and 2000 but opposed Bainimarama's in 2006. In June 2007, the Methodists and the Association of Christian Churches in Fiji sent a letter to Bainimarama declaring their opposition to the planned charter and the council that would draw it up, and reaffirmed their opposition at their annual conference in August 2007.[32] The following year, again at their conference, the church restated that they did not support the charter and said they would begin their own canvassing of villages to gather signatures against it.[33] When I began a new round of fieldwork in December 2008, the church president's office was filled with papers which, I was told, contained 70,000 signatures opposing the charter. The church planned to present them to the nation's president, Ratu Josefa Iloilo, although he was known to be loyal to Bainimarama. But the National Council for Building a Better Fiji preempted the Methodists, handing a final draft of the charter to the president on December 15. At first, the church seemed intent on pressing forward—but the game had already been lost. Ratu Josefa announced that he endorsed the charter, and the church never made its counterpresentation.

Due to the support of the Catholic Archbishop, Petero Mataca, and the prominent activist Father Kevin Barr, the charter might be described loosely as Catholic leaders' response to the Methodist-dominated coups of 1987 and 2000. Narsey wrote sarcastically, "One can understand the satisfaction of the head of the Catholic Church, who having watched for decades, the Methodist Church at the helm of Fiji's leadership, has now done his bit in the sun, to 'take the country forward'. And his clerics will also be happy that 'their' charter proposal for electoral reform will be implemented, whatever the impact the coup has on the rest of the country."[34] However, the Catholic League in Fiji wrote to the pope expressing their unease with the archbishop's political role, and several prominent indigenous Fijian chiefs who are Catholics publicly rejected the charter.[35] It is more accurate, then, to describe the charter as a military government document that received a firm push from the Catholic archbishop to gain traction against Methodist opposition.

When it was first drawn up, the Peoples Charter was seemingly meant to displace ethnonationalist texts of previous decades, such as the pronouncements of "Noqu Kalou, Noqu Vanua" (My God, My Land), a "maxim [that] represents the ideological core around which Fijian ethnonationalist pride revolves" (Ratuva 2002: 21; see also Ryle 2010), and the "Deed of Sovereignty," a manifesto that circulated in the wake of George Speight's coup (Tomlinson 2009: 135–136). But then, either by accident or by design, the charter wound up displacing the very text it was supposedly designed to complement: the constitution. On April 9, 2009, Fiji's appellate court reversed a high court decision from the previous October that had legitimized Bainimarama's takeover of the government. President Iloilo—likely following Bainimarama's orders—quickly abrogated the constitution and reinstated Bainimarama as prime minister (Fraenkel 2010: 421). The Peoples Charter does not function as a constitution, but in the absence of the actual constitution, it became the primary document for mapping out what the government is supposed to do and how it plans to achieve its goals. Brij Lal, who disparages the charter as "a kind of sophomoric development plan," observes that it "has now become the military regime's roadmap, its foundational document, but it is observed more in the breach as the regime tramples upon principles of natural justice and basic human rights in order to entrench itself" (2011: 103, 75). Even as the government ignores the charter's stated principles, however, it expects others to follow them to the letter. In February 2008, looking forward to the following year's planned elections—which were cancelled—the NCBBF's technical director told a journalist, "It is anticipated that the political parties that will contest the March 2009 general election will all have manifestos in which the contents of the Peoples Charter...will dominate."[36]

The charter is meant to be a sign of progress under the military-led government. But for a sign of progress, it can be invoked in detached ways, somewhat reminiscent of Chinese workers' quoting Chairman Mao when getting out of bed in the morning. Consider the case of Fijian fish wardens' use of it:

> Fish wardens are guided by the 11 pillars of the People's Charter for Change and Progress [sic] to prosecute poachers caught in their waters, says fisheries officer Nemani Cavuilati.
>
> Speaking at the Serua district fish wardens refresher course at Namaqumaqua Village on Thursday, Mr Cavuilati said these were the same pillars used by government ministries and departments.
>
> "Even though the Constitution has been abrogated, we are using the pillars of the charter that will enable fish wardens to still carry out their duties and this goes for other departments and units in the Government," Mr Cavuilati said.
>
> Fish warden Saniteri Siga asked fisheries officer Meli Raicebe on the laws now used by the ministry.
>
> He said many poachers were businessman [sic] from Suva and Nausori who were well versed with the law.
>
> Mr Siga said sometimes there were heated arguments when wardens caught poachers.
>
> He said these could end in fights, thus the need for them to be protected by the law.

Mr Raicebe said it was true that the 1997 Constitution has been abrogated but they were now guided by the charter which the Government had given.[37]

It is difficult to say which of the eleven pillars can, realistically, guide the work of fish wardens. One might look to general statements such as "The Public Sector must have established service standards, effective work systems, effective leadership, transparency and accountability and high productivity" (from the explanatory text to pillar number four; NCBBF 2008b: 24). But for authorities like the fisheries officer, the specific pillar does not seem to matter: what matters is the invocation of the Peoples Charter as a kind of holy text—that is, a text that guides and transforms for a higher purpose. It is a shining beacon that lights up itself.

Indeed, the Indo-Fijian scholar Satendra Nandan reportedly described the charter as a sacred text, and, for good measure, compared Bainimarama to Jesus. The co-chair of the NCBBF, Archbishop Petero Mataca, referred to it as a "covenant," a characterization that Bainimarama heartily approved: "I love the remarks he made about the charter being a covenant," he told a journalist in October 2007. "It's an agreement by people who are now alive, people who are dead and the people who are yet to be born."[38] This vision of the charter as a text unifying the living and the dead, as well as the yet-to-be-born, achieves a kind of loony grandeur on the cover of the document itself, which centers the title in a glowing ball of light (Figures 5.2 and 5.3).

I have argued that the Peoples Charter is monologic. This is an argument about ritual textuality's ideology and implementation rather than the details of literary form. In Bakhtinian terms, the Peoples Charter presents multiple voices in dialogue, including a military voice of security, a Catholic voice of social justice, a corporate/bureaucratic voice that speaks of things like "right-sizing" and "e-governance," and the voices of various interest groups that participated in the document's drafting. Such dialogism can be seen as a map of the "transcourse of power" in Fiji, a representation of how people speak with and against other speakers and their anticipated responses in projects of governance (Kaplan and Kelly 1994). The charter presents itself, however, as an icon of unity. It is supposedly an expression of the populace—"we, the people of Fiji"; in reality, it is the expression of a military-led government. As such, it is ultimately a command demanding compliance, with no critical response expected.

FIGURE 5.2 Cover of the Fijian language version of the Peoples Charter.

FIGURE 5.3   Billboard promoting the Peoples Charter, Sigatoka, 2010.

Lend Me Your Ears

Bainimarama's linguistic ideology, as I have illustrated, is a kind of aggressive utopianism in which homology leads to harmony. The Peoples Charter is an attempt to make all citizens read from the same page and say the same things. If people say the same things—so this ideology implies—then Fiji will finally make progress as a nation, moving away from its troubled history of discrimination and violence and toward a future of productive harmony.

Fijian Christians' use of the Bible passage Romans 13:1–2 is an instructive counterexample to this kind of thinking, showing how people may say the same things for different purposes and to different effects. The verses read in part, "there is no power but of God: the powers that be are ordained of God. Whosoever resisteth the power, resisteth the ordinance of God: and they that resist shall receive to themselves damnation." The message might seem simple at first: worldly authorities have been given their authority by God, so political rebellion is contrary to the divine will. In the Fijian context, however, a question immediately arises regarding what kind of authority the verse applies to. British colonialism set up parallel systems of political authority in which chiefly leadership stood alongside multiethnic, bureaucratic, and democratic national government (see especially Clammer 1973; France 1969; Lal 1992; Nayacakalou 1975). When these systems oppose each other, how do Christians know which one has God's blessing?

The Methodist theologian Ilaitia Tuwere wrote about the coups of 1987 and 2000:

The bulk of Fijian Christians of all denominations were unprepared for the moment, not knowing what to say or where to stand in relation to the crisis. The difficulty was also bolstered through interpretation of certain biblical texts in relation to the station of chiefs. This is particularly true of Romans 13:1–2, where reference is made to "supreme authorities" and unmistakably relates to chiefs in the Fijian social system... ([Tuwere back-translates the verse as]: Those who already are chiefs are appointed by God. Whoever rebels against the chief is rebelling against what God has instituted.) Although the translation does not confuse God with the chief, its rendering in the Fijian context gives unequivocal support to the chiefly hierarchy. (Tuwere 2002: 101–102)

Some chiefs, not surprisingly, heartily endorse this interpretation: "When you talk about a chief," said a spokesman for the clan of the paramount chief of Cakaudrove, "you talk about how the Almighty God put leaders in place to lead the *vanua*."[39] As Tuwere makes clear, however, many commoners have also taken this position, endorsing the violence of 1987 and 2000 as a legitimate assertion of Christian chiefly authority against democratic governments. In this reading, then, national government is not counted among "the powers that be." Only chiefs are.

However, at least one prominent evangelist has used the verse to argue the opposite side of the case. This man was Atunaisa Vulaono, a cofounder of the "New Methodist" church and brother of Bainimarama's appointed national police commissioner. In a performance at a public rally in Suva featuring evangelical Christian rugby stars, held in June 2009, Vulaono used Romans 13:1–2 to justify his support for the military-led government (Text 5.1).

Vulaono invokes the Romans passage by observing, "The Bible says those who are chiefs, those who lead are of God" (Kaya na Ivolatabu o era sa turaga tu, ko era sa veiliutaki tu, sa mai vua na Kalou). Note his slippage from "chiefs" to "those who lead"—a movement away from identifying leadership as based exclusively in chiefliness. In the Fijian Bible, as Tuwere notes, the verses refer unambiguously to chiefs; they feature the term for a chief (*turaga*) and do not mention leadership in general (*veiliutaki*) as Vulaono does. The preacher then reaffirms his position in English by declaring, "Romans thirteen, the Bible says Honor those who are in leadership because those in leadership are selected by God." In this segment of his performance, then, Vulaono acrobatically slips away from the Fijian Bible's identification of "chiefs" in Romans 13:1–2 to hold up "leadership" in general, and Bainimarama's leadership in particular, as divinely ordained. Support for Bainimarama necessarily implies a degree of opposition to the chiefly system: recall how he ridiculed the Great Council of Chiefs, saying they should go drink hooch under a mango tree, then suspended and finally abolished the institution. Following this oppositional logic, Vulaono uses the verses on chiefs' divine authority to portray Bainimarama's leadership as legitimate, thereby undercutting the authority of chiefs.

The fact that a wide range of indigenous Fijian Christian speakers finds Romans 13:1–2 relevant and useful means that it has a kind of monologic resonance in which many speakers outwardly say the same thing. But, like those who agree that Fiji suffers from a "coup culture" while

Text 5.1

Original Performance [Mixed Fijian and Fiji-English]	Translation
And I believe, and I believe as a pastor, as I believe as a man of God, it is my duty to take cue from the desire of the leader of the nation. E noqu itavi vakaitalatala na ka e vinakata na ka e vinakata tiko na iliuliu ni matanitu me yacova ko Viti e noqu itavi vakaitalatala meu cakacakataki yau e na vision e vinakata tiko na iliuliu ni matanitu. If not, I'm a rebellion person. Huh? Kevaka iko saqata na ituvatuva ni matanitu iko a rebellion person, go and find another nation. Kaya na Ivolatabu o era sa turaga tu, ko era sa veiliutaki tu, sa mai vua na Kalou.... Kena ibalebale, ke o iko beca, ko beca tiko na Kalou. Veitalia ko lotu, veitalia ko talatala. Veitalia o qase levu, veitalia o qase lailai. Romans thirteen, the Bible says Honor those who are in leadership because those in leadership are selected by God. He promotes, He demotes!	And I believe, and I believe as a pastor, as I believe as a man of God, it is my duty to take my cue from the desire of the leader of the nation. It is my responsibility as a minister, what the leader of the government wants, what he wants for Fiji, it's my responsibility as a minister to make it happen for the vision the leader of the government wants. If not, I'm a rebellious person. Eh? If you are against the government's plans, you are a rebellious person, go and find another nation. The Bible says those who are chiefs, those who lead are from God [that is, ordained as leaders by God].... This means, if you reject, you're rejecting God. Never mind that you go to church, never mind that you're a minister. Never mind that you're the president of the church, never mind that you're a minor official. Romans thirteen, the Bible says Honor those [who] are in leadership because those in leadership are selected by God. He promotes, He demotes!

disagreeing over the events of 2006, speakers who invoke the verses from Romans do so with different voices and different pragmatics, and "it may be that a denotational text...achieves wider acceptance in proportion to its ability to accommodate differing interpretations" (Silverstein and Urban 1996: 14). This point might seem obvious to readers who take it for granted that the Bible can be used to prove anything, but such a dismissal misses two noteworthy facts. First, few verses saturate public consciousness this way. Second, the arbitrary connections that speakers make do not seem arbitrary to the speakers themselves (Jakobson 1990: 411; see also Greenblatt 2010: 16). Particular Bible verses circulate widely because they are thought *not* to be arbitrary or conventional, but to be timeless truths that could have only one interpretation, even as their wide circulation belies the possibility of a single interpretation.[40]

In terms of circulation, the Peoples Charter has not had anything like the scope and force of a text like Chairman Mao's Little Red Book. Not only did Mao's gospel reach hundreds of millions of people, as opposed to the Peoples Charter's hundreds of thousands, but Mao's writ became the ritual basis of a sacralized social order, whereas the charter has not saturated society in the same way.[41] No one considers Bainimarama a Messiah, except perhaps for Bainimarama himself. In presenting the Peoples Charter as a comparative example to Mao's quotations I am not, however, arguing that they have equal effects, but that they have similar patterns of entextualization. Both are monologues. In both cases, one text is meant to circulate at the expense of others. This is the motion of substitution, or, to use a numerical metaphor, the motion of oneness: not oneness in reconciliation, but oneness in erasure.

"To speak dialogically," Webb Keane (2010: 77) writes, "is both to respond to others and to evaluate them in some way." To speak monologically, in contrast, is to evaluate others' speech negatively by treating it (and therefore them) as unrecognizable or essentially nonexistent. As I have argued, the Fijian government led by Voreqe Bainimarama has shown special devotion to monological projects, forbidding criticism while offering new words for speakers to deliver. Like many autocratic leaders, Bainimarama espouses censorship: "at some stage we'll need to shut some people up," as he put it memorably. This censorship is meant to serve a coercive but creative project: a single-voiced, straight-line path of textual movement through public space, leading finally to "we, the people" united in progress.

6

Full Stop

HOW DO PEOPLE shape their own expectations and evaluations of what counts as an effective ritual performance? To begin to answer this question, in this book I have approached ritual as a tendency toward entextualization, in which discourse is made into object-like signs and texts arranged in specific patterns. The patterns I have examined are sequence, conjunction, contrast, and substitution. In the ethnography presented here, these patterns are interactively created by participants at a wide range of events, from a hyperactive Pentecostal crusade to quiet kava-drinking sessions, from nineteenth-century deathbeds to the twenty-first century projects of a military-led government. In each case, I have examined how beliefs about motion shape people's practices, including beliefs about how moving one's body in exuberant worship compels God to join you, how following the rules of kava drinking places a person on an immovable foundation, how dying the right way sends a person to heaven while building God's kingdom on earth, and how speaking with one voice can ensure social progress, the metaphorical movement of growth toward a better future.

In this conclusion, I return to the four patterns of entextualization, discussing related but distinct varieties in order to show that the approach I have taken does not set limits on a closed-off system. Typologies are dead things. (And, following fractal logic, *dead* dead things—but there it is, more typologizing!) Rather, I hope to open up new areas for exploration within the study of ritual textuality and ritual performance more broadly.

In the discussion of sequences in Chapter 2, I followed the performative paths of a Pentecostal preacher's sermon and altar call, showing how he wove a rhetorical pattern of declarations, promises, and actions

which helped inspire and physically move his audience as they sought salvation. Another kind of sequence can be called *repetition*, the reinvocation
of an event through time as contexts change. This is seen in indigenous
Fijian attention to "curses" which do not go away despite repeated ritual
intervention. The best-known curse haunts a village in the highlands of
Vitilevu where Methodist missionary Thomas Baker and seven members
of his traveling party were killed in 1867. In 1903, members of the village
presented a whale's tooth in apology to the Methodist Synod because they
believed they were cursed as a result of the massacre. At the time, they felt
their apology had been successful, and "their fathers' sin had been expi-
ated" (Wood 1978: 164). In 1985, however, they apologized again, this time
with an elaborate procession in which they carried a lit torch and a whale's
tooth to Suva for the Methodist Church's one hundred fiftieth anniversary
in Fiji. Then in 2003, villagers held yet another ritual apology, this time
inviting Baker's descendants, because they felt "the curse had not been
lifted and its effects—problematic relations with local government, lack
of development, social problems, infertile land and bad harvests—continued to dominate their lives" (Ryle 2010: 71). This third apology had strong
Pentecostal involvement, highlighting newer denominations' influence
in convincing indigenous Fijians that land is cursed, a topic to which
I return later.[1]

The curse of the Reverend Baker, in short, is not going away; villagers have ritually returned to it three times within a century. I am calling
this pattern "repetition" because of the repeated invocation of an original event—a metaphorical cycling back—which bypasses earlier engage-
ments with that original event. In other words, the later events in the
sequence refer primarily to the original event (here, the murder of the
Baker party) rather than to each other. As performances, the 1903 apology, the 1985 apology, and the 2003 apology featured different participants
with different individual motivations, changed historical circumstances,
and also presumably different fears about what, specifically, the curse was
now causing to happen. For many people in 2003, the situation of 1903
would undoubtedly look like a golden age when chiefs were powerful, kinship bonds were stronger, and problems like marijuana cultivation did not
afflict the highlands.

The practice of apologizing for curses is now a general one in Fiji.
Although Baker's is the most famous and best-documented case, many
villages and families have their own stories about how their forefathers'
sins and bad intentions linger and need to be resolved, and leaders at

the Methodist Church's annual national conference often receive ceremonial apologies meant to extinguish curses.[2] Pentecostals and evangelicals
offer their own versions of Christianity as ways to escape, at last, the spiral
of repetition in which Methodists are trapped (Ryle 2010). In emphasizing
the reality of curses, however, such groups give them a jolt of adrenaline
in discourse and practice. Rather than make curses go away, Pentecostal
and evangelical groups make them even more present and frightening, as
shown by the case of the man with "vision" from the Holy Spirit who saw
the demon in Kadavu, described in Chapter 4.

For the pattern of conjunction, I analyzed chiasmus in Fijian
kava-drinking sessions and compared it with Christian communion.
A pattern of conjunction distinct from chiasmus is *parallelism*, which
keeps terms aligned without crossing. In parallelism, terms are joined
but kept distinct. Parallelism is very well represented in studies of ritual
language, and featured in Chapter 2 in the discussion of the preacher
Kenneth Colegrove's sermon and altar call. In Fijian Methodism, a prominent example of parallelism is the pairing of the terms *vanua* (land,
people, and chiefdoms) and *lotu* (Christianity). As an indigenous Fijian
anthropologist puts it, "The *vanua* and the Methodist church are regarded
as inseparable by most Methodist church members" (Degei 2007: vi).
Their inseparability is prominent in public discourse, where the two
terms are often aligned. For example, in September 1998, the superintendent minister of Kadavu preached a sermon in which he asked, "Who
leads? The *lotu* or the *vanua*? Who should be leading? The *lotu* or the
vanua? I should confirm one thing: forget the word '*lotu*'; forget the word
'*vanua*'. We can say the *lotu* is behind; the *vanua* is behind; God alone
leads."[3] Often, *lotu* and *vanua* are joined with *matanitu*, meaning "government," but as I have argued elsewhere, government is a comparatively weak third term, evoking little of the passion of the first two terms
(Tomlinson 2009: 23–24).

Webb Keane has argued that "in the juxtapositions created by parallelism each line can serve as figure and ground by turn. The couplet as
a whole...appears to be a metaphor for a third term" (Keane 1997: 108).
Although he is writing about poetic couplets in Sumba, Indonesia, and
Fijians do not have a similar oratorical tradition, Keane's observation fits
indigenous Fijian Methodist usage of *lotu* and *vanua* well: the terms are
used to frame each other, and, taken together, they define a third object,
namely indigeneity. In other words, for many Fijian Methodists, *lotu* and

vanua are the two things that go together to mark a distinctly indigenous identity.

In Chapter 4, I turned to nineteenth-century deathbed scenes to explain fractal recursivity as a pattern of contrast—in that case, the mutually implicated contrasts of life/death and public/private. Another pattern of contrast can be called *polarization*, in which a single sign or text is metaphorically divided against itself and the parts are "pushed" in opposite evaluative directions. (It recalls Batesonian schismogenesis, the process of "progressive differentiation"; Bateson 1935: 181.) The transformation of the term *vanua* is a good example. As discussed at length in Chapter 3, *vanua* means both "land" and "people" and connotes the traditional order under the authority of chiefs. Over the past several decades, the term has become polarized by being defined in one direction as the inherently good foundation of indigenous Fijians' collective identity, and in the other direction as the inherently bad location of demonic influence that thwarts their efforts and holds them back.

Several decades ago, authors wrote of the *vanua* in dispassionate terms of land and social organization. In the works of mid-century scholars such as Rusiate Nayacakalou, Peter France, and Cyril Belshaw, the *vanua* was a unit of social organization usually defined as a collection of *yavusa* (sometimes translated "clan"), which in turn incorporated units called *mataqali* which the colonial government designated as primary landholding units. In these writers' accounts, social organization was shown to be flexible and regionally diverse, and local practices often did not match colonial categories. Still, there was a general sense of Fijian society being built from the bottom up, with smaller groups coalescing—at least temporarily—into larger ones. These larger-level groups gained a kind of effectiveness that lower-level groups lacked. For example, Nayacakalou argued that "It is really at the level of the *vanua* that chieftainship begins to emerge clearly as a definite institution" (1975: 37; see also Nayacakalou 1978: 147), and Belshaw wrote, "The main strengths of the vanua are that it contains organizational experience, and that it is sufficiently large to command resources and personnel" (1964: 277). In this kind of scholarship, the *vanua* was present and important but did not have the status of something that unites all Fijians. It was not, in a word, foundational. Rather, it was an end product.

In comparison, recent indigenous Fijian scholarship has tended to treat the *vanua* as the beginning of all things. The anthropologist Asesela

Ravuvu offers a remarkable passage that begins with a dry definition of the *vanua* as a social unit—a definition whose flexible generality would have appealed to Nayacakalou—but then moves into religious rhapsody:

> The *vanua*, in the sense of the largest grouping of kinsmen who are structured into a number of social units which are related to one another, is the living soul or human manifestation of the physical environment which the members have since claimed to belong to them and to which they also belong.... Like the interdependence of the body and the soul, the people control and decide what happens to the land. However, the people cannot live without the physical embodiment in terms of their land. The land is the physical or geo-graphical entity of the people, upon which their survival as individuals and as a group depends. It is a major source of life; it provides nourishment, shelter and protection. It is a source of security and provides the material basis for identity and belonging. Land is thus an extension of the self. Likewise the people are an extension of the land. (Ravuvu 1983: 76)

The difference between Nayacakalou and Ravuvu, Fiji's first two professional indigenous anthropologists, is remarkable: the former treats the *vanua* as just one kind of social unit, and the latter treats it as *the* social unit, the origin of all else.[4] This second understanding of the *vanua* also informs the work of Ilaitia Tuwere, the theologian and former president of the Methodist Church of Fiji whom I have quoted at length in Chapters 3 and 5. Tuwere has written a nuanced book-length account of the theological dimensions of the *vanua* in which he echoes Ravuvu's line about body and soul, and explores aspects of the *vanua* as mother, garden, and gift. Finally, the education scholar Unaisi Nabobo-Baba calls for a methodological approach to Fijian studies which she labels "vanua research," presenting the *vanua* itself as the key to understanding Fijian social dynamics rather than the reverse (Tuwere 2002; Nabobo-Baba 2006a; see also Manoa 2010; Seruvakula 2000).

Considered a divine gift that God gave exclusively to indigenous Fijians, and fetishized as something that can act upon people (Tomlinson 2009: 141), the *vanua* was the political emblem that mobilized popular support for the coups of 1987 and 2000.[5] But some Pentecostal and evangelical Christians have begun to dissent, viewing it not as the rock of existence but as a pit of demons. In their view, the land is haunted by non-Christian spirits. To live healthily and prosperously in the present, people need to turn to God in order to wipe out these malign influences that infect the soil. A group called the Evangelical Fellowship has led efforts at "healing the land," which the anthropologist Lynda Newland identifies as their "core project" (2007: 307). She quotes one evangelical leader's summary of their work: "They go out to the village and get all the villagers...look at their problems, do a spiritual mapping, map out where the devil has been influential—whether it's a killing field in one place or it's where they worshipped demons in the past—and then they cleanse those out" (2007: 307; see also Pigliasco 2010, 2012; Ryle 2010). This kind of practice—"spiritual warfare" against soil wormy with demons—focuses intensely on local sites, but as a plan of action it can be applied anywhere. In July 2006, a land-healing squad from Fiji traveled to Nunavut in the Canadian Arctic to participate in earth-cleansing rituals there (Laugrand and Oosten 2007).[6]

As I noted in Chapter 1, patterns of entextualization intersect, and the term *vanua* moves in ways besides polarization. For example, as I mentioned earlier, it complements *lotu* in parallelism, and as I argued in Chapter 3, its double meaning as land and people orients the chiasmus of kava-drinking sessions. Here, my purpose is simply to observe how polarization is distinct from fractal recursivity as a pattern of contrast, and has its own implications for ritual performance. *Vanua* has become solemn in a way that was not evident in the literature on Fiji from half a century ago, and that solemnity has been moving toward a romantic glorification of *vanua* in one direction and toward a demonization of it in the other.

For the fourth pattern, substitution, I focused on monologue. Living in Bainimarama's Fiji, it was hard not to. Another kind of substitution, which can be called *refinement*, also deserves attention. In this pattern, particular signs are replaced within a text in order to change the way the whole text circulates and is taken up. In contemporary Fiji, refinement is seen in two competing projects of Bible translation. One project aims to make the text older and one aims to make it newer. The historian Andrew Thornley has spearheaded the first project, a revival of the New Testament translations of Methodist missionary John Hunt from the 1840s. Hunt's version was revised poorly by James Calvert in the 1850s, and the current standard translation in Fiji is Frederick Langham's effort of 1902. The purpose of the new translation, as explained in its Fijian-language introduction, is "not to replace the New Testament that we use today. It is simply hoped that we can also read the book that Hunt worked so hard on, so we can see how good his translation is"; it also notes that Hunt "translated directly from Greek to Fijian" (Thornley, Tuwere, and Vulaono 2007: 6, 5).[7] Ilaitia Tuwere, one of Thornley's partners in the project, told me in an interview in 2007, "I may sound old-fashioned, you know, wanting to go back to John Hunt's translation. But it's not simply because it's old…but [it's] to be opened and to be studied and get back to some of the words that have been lost."[8]

Moving sharply in the other direction, a team funded by the evangelical Christian businessman and politician James Ah Koy produced a "New Fijian Translation" in 2010. This is a Bible translation that ultimately depends on changing a single word. Ah Koy criticized the standard interpretation (both in the Bible and in everyday speech) of the word *kalougata* as meaning "blessing." *Kalou* means "god" or "spirit," and *gata* means two things: (1) sharp or effective, and (2) a snake. As "blessing," *kalougata* incorporates the first sense of *gata* to convey spiritual effectiveness. However, if one draws on the definition of *gata* as snake, as Ah Koy does, one gets the sinister term "snake-godded" (see also Tuwere 2002: 137).

In the Fijian pantheon, a deity named Degei "ranks as supreme among the gods" and appears as a snake, or "with the head and part of the body of that reptile, the rest of his form being stone, emblematic of everlasting and unchangeable duration" (Williams 1982 [1858]: 217). Ah Koy came to believe that when Fijians say *kalougata* in blessing each other, or read it in the Bible, they are actually cursing each other by invoking Degei. His solution was to have the Bible translation fixed, and his New Fijian Translation team replaced *kalougata* throughout the Bible with *kalouvinaka*, literally "good god"; thus the act of blessing is "good-godding." The translators made other changes, too, but it was Ah Koy's discomfort with the semantic slippage between effectiveness and snakes that set the project in motion.[9]

Refinement, as I am defining it, is limited and partial. Thornley, Tuwere, and Ah Koy evidently revere the Bible and do not want to change it as a whole, but to correct what they consider to be man-made errors of translation and to recover original meanings. As a pattern, it involves a switch within a text—Hunt's words for Langham's, *kalouvinaka* for *kalougata*—that is meant to prompt new dissemination of that text through public space.

In Fiji, the distinct patterns of sequence, conjunction, contrast, and substitution have articulated projects in which participants seek salvation by shouting it, locate themselves in an eternal homeland by drinking it, die in a happy way by saying it, and attempt to make others speak in a single, unanswerable voice. In analyzing patterns of entextualization, I have attempted to give ethnographic substance to metaphors of motion, keying this attempt to the question of ritual efficacy—how people shape their own expectations and evaluations of what counts as an effective ritual performance. I have argued that a theory of ritual textuality requires close attention to semiotic ideologies—that is, what people think signs are and how they work. By taking this approach, I am pushing the well-worn metaphor of motion in a semiotic direction. I have also shown how ritual participants draw on broader ideas about motion, ideas that go beyond patterns of entextualization. In the Chapter 2 analysis of Kenneth Colegrove's sermon and altar call, I observed how he characterized physical motion as the key to a successful performance. If his audience bounced their bodies, clapped, and thrust their hands to heaven while yelling praise, they would make the Holy Ghost fall on Albert Park, into their very bodies, speaking ecstatically through them. In the discussion of kava-drinking sessions in Chapter 3, I noted the crucial distinction between the two main senses of the Fijian term *vanua*—as land, the *vanua* stays still; as people, the *vanua* moves—which orients the logic of chiasmus by which these sessions become acts of communion. For the Methodist missionaries described in Chapter 4, negotiations of the boundaries between life and death, and public and private, created a double sense of progress: progress for the mission that was winning souls, and progress for those souls that were now headed to heaven instead of to the Fijian afterworld of Burotu. Finally, the officials discussed in Chapter 5—coup leader Bainimarama and his supporters—also share ideologies of progress, tied in this case to projects of monologue. If everyone will stop criticizing the government and instead say what the government tells them to, Bainimarama and his associates insist, the nation will finally move ahead into a stable and secure future, finally free of "coup culture."

To understand how rituals succeed or fail, then, the motion of ritual textuality matters in two ways. First, it matters when people create distinct patterns in order to achieve particular results: bringing divinity and humanity into semiotic communion, for example, or muting the echo box of critical discourse so that a nation's citizens fall into monological line. Second, it matters when people articulate semiotic and textual patterns with broader ideologies of motion—what counts as motion, how to recognize it, how to generate it, and what its consequences are: the conviction that God arrives when congregations move their bodies and make joyful noise, or the certainty that a mission's progress is to be located most finely on people's deathbeds. In all of the examples offered in this book, these two ways come together in those moments when people interactively confront the question of how to perform ritual effectively. Sometimes rituals are quiet, routine affairs, the endless procession of kava cups served on a drowsy night. Sometime rituals fail: Bainimarama's monologues have divided and damaged Fiji, not united or healed it. But at their most compelling, rituals can generate their own aura of powerful inevitability, smoothness shining through halts and gaps to make events themselves seem to move, drawing people, words, and things together in a full and faithful completion.

Notes

1. For these terms and characterizations, see Appadurai (1996, 2006), Tsing (1995), Ortner (2006: 18), Clifford (1997), and Urban (2001, 2010), respectively. The fact that motion is now a dominant metaphor does not, it must be emphasized, mean that earlier understandings of culture were necessarily static or inert.

2. Two caveats are necessary. The first is that the distinction between performance and performativity needs to be kept clearly in mind. Performance is "the assumption of responsibility to an audience for a display of communicative skill, highlighting the way in which communication is carried out, above and beyond its referential content" (Bauman 1986: 3). Performativity, as described earlier, is the force of speech acts. As Kulick puts it, with reference to both Austin and Judith Butler, "performance is something a subject does. Performativity, on the other hand, is the process through which the subject emerges" (Kulick 2003: 140). Not all performances include performative acts except in a trivial sense, and the role of an audience in conditioning a statement's performative force is contextually variable. Failure to distinguish between the terms leads to conceptual confusion as seen in Bell's criticism of performance theory (Bell 1992: 37–46). The second caveat is that connections between performative language and notions of ritual efficacy are never determinative or exclusive, as shown by scholars such as Ahern (1979), Gardner (1983), Robbins (2001b), and Tambiah (1985 [1979]). Robbins observes how paying attention to Austin's distinction between illocutionary force (the act in saying something) and perlocutionary force (that which follows as a consequence) "frees analysts from having to distinguish between linguistic utterances that are 'actions' and those that are only 'statements'" (Robbins 2001b: 593 n. 4)—the kind of distinction that Bell (1992) notably

criticized in studies of ritual. In avoiding the misleading division between action and representation while attending to the differences between illocutionary and perlocutionary force, analysts can gain insights into the ways people expect ritual language to achieve its effects (Robbins 2001b: 594). In this regard, while I have been influenced by Schieffelin's writings on ritual performance, especially his attention to performance's contingent, emergent qualities, I disagree with his argument that "performance can never be text," which falsely treats texts as static, indeed "changeless" things with single authors (Schieffelin 1998: 198).

3. On this point, I am drawing inspiration from Richard Parmentier's work on history in Palau. Parmentier notes that Palauan discourse and practice feature four key icons: paths, sides, cornerposts, and degrees of size. The first three can be conceptualized numerically: paths contain a single element, sides contain two opposed and balanced elements, and cornerposts contain four interrelated elements. Paths are sequences, such as sacred stones that mark points on an ancestor's voyage. Sides are relationships of opposition and balance, implying complementarity and reciprocity. Finally, cornerposts are four-part relationships in which the parts have distinct functions and positions in a hierarchy but work together as a unit, such as a village's four chiefs. To simplify Parmentier's argument, cornerposts have a degree of vulnerability to historical transformation that paths do not. They mark developments in order and hierarchy, but later political changes can "skew" the iconic structure, and "social categories or institutions organized by cornerpost relations tend to become reduced to sides in the face of imposed social changes," such as the introduction of colonial rule (Parmentier 1987: 122, 118). In comparison, paths "tend to be self-perpetuating"; people maintain paths by keeping the nodes symbolically active even when they no longer really exist, as when "abandoned houses are still formally invited to attend social events, and titles are still awarded to men who rule over nonexistent social units" (1987: 116). Parmentier argues that in actual practice, these icons "occur in complexes, either the multiplication of one diagram (intersecting paths, overlaid cornerposts) or the interpenetration of different models," and that semiotic complexity is generally not fully accessible to most people's awareness (1987: 113; see also Silverstein 1981).

4. These names are listed among the "Top 10 Dive Sites" on www.divekadavu.com, accessed February 27, 2013.

5. See *Fiji Sun*, April 24, 2009, p. 6.

CHAPTER 2

1. Colegrove preached with a heavy Texas accent, which I do not reproduce here except for his distinctive use of "wisht" for present-tense "wish," a common

feature of southern US pronunciation (see Brown 1891: 172).

2. Unlike the sermon, the altar call was translated into Fijian. In this chapter, I focus on Colegrove's English delivery; see Tomlinson (2012a) for a discussion of the dynamics of translation during the altar call. Many indigenous Fijians understand English well and are familiar with biblical themes, and the audience responded to Colegrove's English-language statements during the sermon with claps and cheers at the appropriate moments. This leads me to believe that most audience members followed Colegrove's sermon and had little difficulty comprehending it.

3. In these transcriptions from the crusade, words in parentheses are ones that are difficult to hear clearly on the recording but about whose utterance I am reasonably certain.

4. On learning glossolalia, see De Witte (2011), Goodman (1972), Luhrmann (2012), Samarin (1972), and Tomlinson (2012a).

5. I am borrowing the term "prospective momentum" from Miyazaki (2004).

6. On God's agency as "an assumed background against which the person acts or seeks divine sources for the radical assertion of the individual's own agency," see Keane (2007: 208–209 n. 6).

7. I have examined parts of Laveasiga's sermon for different purposes in Tomlinson (2009).

8. The philosopher and theologian Nicholas Wolterstorff compares promises and commands by observing, "What promising introduces is the (*prima facie*) right of the addressee to hold the speaker to it; what commanding introduces is the (*prima facie*) right of the speaker to hold the addressee to it" (1995: 34–35). By continually moving from promises (and other future-oriented statements) to actions which frequently include commands, Colegrove therefore sets up a dynamic give-and-take of responsibility in which both performer and audience continually and co-constructively fulfill obligations to each other.

9. The ellipses in Arno's text indicate drawn-out syllables.

10. The ultimate evidence of ritual efficacy in this case, then, would be whether people considered themselves saved—but there is a catch: "It is...one of the ingenious design features of many kinds of Christianity that they make the ever-renewed conviction of sinfulness an important condition of salvational success.... So what is most important is not eradicating sin completely but trying earnestly to avoid it as much as possible and then responding to it with contrition when, as it inevitably does, it occurs" (Robbins 2004: 252).

CHAPTER 3

1. After the first cup, several other cups are drunk by church authorities, including other priests and the cross bearer, but individual members of the congregation

do not drink. In a footnote, McGrath adds: "It is custom to drink the cup in the name of another. The priest drinks it in the name of God, and the cross-bearer in the name of the community. In the liturgy of the Eucharist a member of the community drinks the cup in the name of all" (McGrath 1973: 66 n. 6). Although McGrath does not specify in the last sentence that the cup drunk "in the name of all" for the Eucharist is wine, not kava, this is almost certainly the case. See also Wright (1979: 41) for an account of an ecumenical worship service in Tonga in which pounded kava and cut-up sugarcane were identified with Christ's punished body and then served to all.

2. In early Christianity, some groups rejected the use of wine in the Eucharist: "in the second and third centuries, if not already in the first, a number of more or less heretical groups took exception to the use of wine and celebrated their eucharists in bread alone or in bread and salt; or if they retained the cup, it contained only water" (Dix 1945: 48).

3. The metaphor comes from the Bible. For example, 1 Corinthians 12:12–27 reads in part, "For as the body is one, and hath many members, and all the members of that one body, being many, are one body: so also is Christ. For by one Spirit are we all baptized into one body.... Now ye are the body of Christ, and members in particular"; Colossians 1:18 states that Christ "is the head of the body, the church."

4. For pointing out chiasmus's cross-modal characteristics and their implications, I thank Kristina Wirtz.

5. Besides being subverted, communion can fail. An intriguing example comes from the Wiru of Papua New Guinea, described in Clark (2000: 160–161). Wesleyan church members believe they must take communion to get to heaven. So they do—but it leaves them hungry and they wonder why "if spirits are satisfied with what they are offered [in traditional sacrifice], why then does communion not fill their bellies? These statements are literal and metaphorical and refer to the fact that communion is not seen to work" (161). Clark explains that in taking communion, Wiru not only want to become good Christians, but also "to become 'like whites.'" "These metamorphoses have begun," he notes, "but they are by no means complete and many Wiru remain pessimistic as to the final outcome" (161). At one level, Wiru communion "works," in the sense that people feel they must practice it, and do so to try to get to heaven. But Clark's broader argument is that the ritual continually fails, as it never really accomplishes what Wiru want it to.

6. "Remote Oceania" (as well as its counterpart, "near Oceania") is a term used by archaeologists in preference to the categories of Melanesia, Micronesia, and Polynesia (Green 1991; Kirch 1997). The terms "near" and "remote" refer to migration and settlement histories, and "remote" does not have any pejorative connotation in this usage.

7. There are two notable exceptions to land's fixity. The first comes from mining, as fragments of territories get sent around the world. As Katerina Teaiwa

points out, places that have been mined intensively for phosphate like Nauru and Banaba disrupt simplistic equations of place and identity: "Who belongs to the Banaban soil that was dispersed across the New Zealand landscape? Could Banabans come to New Zealand or Australia and feel 'at home'?" (K. Teaiwa 2005: 187; see also T. Teaiwa 1998). The second exception is legends of places like Burotu, "a mythological island where the spirits go and enjoy themselves forever" or an "invisible island inhabited only by beautiful young virgins" (Ratuvili 1971: 87; Baleiwaqa 1987: 1) The Methodist missionary Thomas Williams wrote that in Burotu, "there is an abundance of all that a native deems most to be desired" (Williams 1982 [1858]: 247; see also Hale 1968 [1846]: 56; Waterhouse 1997 [1866]: 290); thus to say "'I am in Burotu' means 'I am thoroughly contented'" (Geraghty 1993: 347). The key point is that Burotu is not a solid, visible, terrestrial thing, but an elusive one: it is "located under the sea" (Thompson 1940: 115) or it "floats around the Fiji group unseen by navigators" (Heatley 1923: 10). Hocart quotes an informant who asserts that Burotu "lies within the sea, and is not seen above. If it is about to emerge at any place and a boat is in the offing, it sinks again; if it sinks the swirl of it rises up" (1929: 195). Paul Geraghty, who has written the definitive account, observes that "All Fijian sources state that Burotu is now submerged, and periodically re-emerges" (1993: 360; see also Nunn 2009: 163–168). Floating islands like Burotu are an exception that proves the rule, otherworldly lands moving in contrast to other *vanua* that are fixed in place. I discuss Burotu further in Chapter 4 in regard to Fijian narratives about the afterlife.

8. Although land does not move, this does not mean it is inactive. It can be described as a living thing, and if violated it can "bite" (Dickhardt 2000: 260). Because of its spiritual vibrancy—both as the home of indigenous spiritual presence and as God's gift to faithful Christians—land is *mana*, or effective. But to say that the *vanua* can act is not the same thing as saying that it is in motion.

9. Regarding immobile (sitting) paramount chiefs, Sahlins is writing specifically of the Roko Tui Dreketi of Rewa; he notes that Basil Thomson "considered Rewa 'the most perfect [i.e., paradigmatic] example of a Fijian state known to us'" (2004: 57). Building on the work of Hocart, Sahlins notes that the distinction between mobile and immobile chiefs broke down in colonial Fiji, with paramount chiefs becoming "so...exalted...as to upset the old balance of paired groups....The two sides that used to face each other...have begun to break up into units which all face the chief, like planets around the sun" (Hocart quoted in Sahlins 2004: 61; see also Thomas 1986).

10. Nawalowalo was the chairman of both the Fiji Kava Council and the International Kava Executive Council. I interviewed him on January 3, 2006, in Tavuki. Our conversation was in mixed Fijian (both Standard Fijian and Kadavuan) and English.

11. I interviewed him on January 16, 2006, in Nagonedau village. Our conversation was in Fijian.

12. "The drunkenness hits you" is my translation of *yacova ke mai ke na majeni*, which might be phrased more literally as "drunkenness happens."

13. *Tabu Kaisi*, which I am translating as "No Peasants," is also the name of a kind of mat woven for chiefs. Grimshaw (1907: 102) translated the name as "forbidden to commoners," which conveys the sense of prohibition indicated by *tabu* (taboo), but underplays the insult of *kaisi*, a term for people with no land. A Fijian monolingual dictionary defines *kaisi* as *tamata toro-sobu duadua*, meaning "lowest person" (Tabana ni Vosa kei Na iTovo Vakaviti 2005: 215).

    In the final stages of preparing this book manuscript, I became dissatisfied with the translation of *kaisi* as "peasant(s)" because no one really uses "peasant" as an insult in modern English. For advice I turned to "Apo" Aporosa of Hamilton, New Zealand, who has an extensive electronic network of Fijian friends, and asked him for people's opinions on what would be an appropriate translation of *kaisi*. In the seven responses received, two people mentioned "swine," two suggested "bastard," and a third intensified it as "low-down dirty bastard." One mentioned "low-class," another mentioned "low-born and of low rank," and yet another said "a real low-life type person."

14. See Arno (1990, 1993) for analysis of forms of talk at kava sessions, and Brison (2007) for discussion of the public representation of *vanua* identities in kava ceremonies, including ideologies of local versus national-standard dialect use. See also Abramson (2005: 328) for a discussion of how kava drinking has become an emblem of indigenous Fijian ethnicity heavily marketed by the tourist industry, offered in ceremonies "from which ancestral and divine powers have been extracted."

15. It is commonly stated that women did not drink kava in earlier days, but I have argued elsewhere that this is generally a misrepresentation (see Tomlinson 2009: 126; compare Herr 1983: 77, 246). The historical dissonance becomes poetic harmony in Teresia K. Teaiwa's comment, "we drank so much [kava] that day. i never realised fijian women drank so much [kava], what grog swipers! i felt like i was drowning in those muddy waters, drinking from ten a.m. to ten p.m." (1998: 102).

16. There is a wide range of contextual variability to how people are ranked. Still, there is a degree of robustness to the system: certain people always sit comparatively high in the circle, and certain people reliably sit low. Christina Toren has written extensively on the ways in which kava ceremonies interconvert relations of hierarchy with relations of balanced reciprocity; see especially Toren (1988, 1990, 1999).

17. Unlike alcohol, however, kava does not generally change one's state of mind. Indeed, Michael W. Young, writing of Vanuatu, suggests "the meditative

and quietistic effects of kava are conducive to a *protestant* understanding of Christianity, especially to the central notion of Communion.... Would it have been any different if the missionaries had tried honestly to penetrate the mysteries of kava, and solicited its use to communicate and teach their own religious mysteries?" (Young 1995: 75).

18. I interviewed him in Fijian on January 24, 2006, in Nagonedau.

19. On this painting, see Ryle (2010: 23–26). Another work of art combining the symbolism of kava and Christian communion with a neo-traditional twist is Epeli Hau'ofa's poem "Blood in the Kava Bowl" (1980). The verses describe a foreign professor who talks to kava drinkers about their "oppression," but, Hau'ofa writes, "he tastes not the blood in the kava / mixed with dry waters that rose to Tangaloa / who gave us the cup from which we drink / the soul and the tears of our land."

   At the Pacific Theological College, Samoan students have been most explicit in discussing kava drinking's Eucharistic logic. A master of theology thesis written by a student from the Congregational Christian Church of Samoa states: "The sacramental act of the [kava] Ceremony reveals that every time the ceremony is enacted, the chiefs participat[ing] in the ceremony know that *at that moment* they are in communion with their God in Christ" (Faleali'i 1998: 101; emphasis in original). Another Samoan student, a Methodist, drew parallels between kava's preparation and Jesus' crucifixion: "The pounded [kava] can be interpreted as a symbol of the Christ who was crushed on the cross. From the cross His blood (the liquid [kava]) was poured out to redeem, reconcile and unify the world as God's people" (Fa'asi'i 1993: 63; see also Taofinu'u 1995).

20. I interviewed him in English. In this quotation, I have made minor edits for clarity while trying to maintain his unique voice. For example, I have deleted some repetitions, false starts, and placeholders; the text's meaning is not altered.

CHAPTER 4

1. Webb (1870: 204).

2. The sociologist Andrew Abbott observes how such calibrations can lead to disciplinary misunderstanding in the social sciences, where homologous positions are likely to be misread as identical ones. "If I tell you I am a positivist," he writes, "you in fact know only that in my usual domain of interaction most people I deal with are more interpretive than I. Unless you can already identify that usual domain of interaction, you don't really know anything more than you knew before I spoke. Relative to you, I might be strongly interpretive" (Abbott 2001: 12).

3. Regarding the strangling of widows, Christine Weir has written that "there is a sense in which the women were at least partial agents in the ritual" (1998: 159).

4. For a thorough consideration of changing Western representations of, and attitudes toward, death and dying from the medieval era to the present, see Ariès (1981). For a universal definition of a good death—"one which suggests some degree of mastery over the arbitrariness of the biological occurrence by replicating a prototype to which all such deaths conform, and which can therefore be seen as an instance of a general pattern necessary for the reproduction of life"—see Bloch and Parry (1982: 15).

5. The term he used for "removed" was likely *toki*. Second Corinthians 5:1 reads: "For we know that if our earthly house of this tabernacle were dissolved, we have a building of God, an house not made with hands, eternal in the heavens."

6. Some accounts of happy deaths focus on the dying person's beliefs (spoken aloud, of course) that there was a proper location where one should die and be buried as a good Christian. For example, the paramount chief of Naceva in Kadavu reportedly "besought Joeli [Nau, a Tongan minister], saying, 'Joeli, if you are my true friend, do not let me be buried in the place where the old chiefs and my friends will wish to inter me, but let my corpse be buried in *that spot* in the chapel where I sat, and heard that sermon which pierced my soul'" (Webb 1870: 204, emphasis in original). Evidently, the chief believed that the traditional burial ground was the wrong place for his mortal remains, and he wanted them interred in the site where he felt a wounding certainty of new faith. As another example, Paula Vea, a Tongan who was one of the most successful early Methodist missionaries in Kadavu, insisted on dying in Fiji. As he lay ill in Kadavu, he recalled that "My friends have frequently pressed me of late to return to Tonga, my own land; but I always told them that I had given myself for life to the work of God in Fiji, and my mind is made up to die at my post in Fiji"; the missionary who recorded this account added, "And the thought that he had been enabled to resist all their pleadings was no small source of joy to him at last" (White 1867b: 610).

7. Earlier in his life, when Ratu Cakobau resisted Christianity, he had explicitly rejected the Wesleyan ideal of the happy death. The historian Andrew Thornley, working from the original journals of missionary William Cross, recounts:

Cakobau [in November 1839] conceded that other parts of Fiji might well accept Christianity but [the chiefdom of] Bau would not do so. Cross responded (as he had with other chiefs) by pronouncing the inevitability, as told in Scripture, of Christianity's victory. Even if Cakobau did not become Christian, his children would, added Cross, to which Cakobau vowed that when he died he would command his children not to convert. Cross then graphically described the everlasting torment facing Cakobau beyond death. Confronted with the journey of the soul, Cakobau simply said, "this dying is the thing which is difficult." (Thornley 2005: 339)

8. I have back-translated from the Fijian version. See also Tomlinson (2006a: 136–138); Toren (2004: 232–233). People could, of course, refuse to die the way the mission wanted them to. A striking example comes from Mary Wallis's diary entries of May and June 1847. She was a trader's wife, not a missionary, but she strongly supported the mission's efforts, and the publication of her diaries was endorsed by the Reverend James Calvert (Wallis 1851: iii–v). Reporting on the sickness and death of a German sailor named Bernardo H. Bloom, Wallis characterized him as "very irritable and impatient, cursing and swearing because the Almighty does not cure him, or take his life." On the tenth of May, Wallis described a conversation she had with him:

> I asked him to-day if he felt prepared to die, knowing that he had given up all hope of life. He said he supposed he was. I asked him if he read his Bible. He replied that he did. I told him if he did, he knew what constituted a Christian character, and asked him if he believed that he was a Bible Christian, and if he was conscious of loving and serving God. His reply was in the affirmative, and he added, "I never sinned much. God is merciful. He will not send me to hell for the few sins that I have committed." "I know nothing of your life," I replied, "except that since you have been on board this vessel you have been exceedingly profane; and even since your sickness, you have uttered oaths enough to sink your soul in everlasting misery." "Oh, I can repent of that easy enough," was his reply. I conversed with him some time longer, but his mind appeared so completely blinded, that he could not be convinced he was a sinner, or needed the pardoning grace of God. Some of the sailors were present, and he would look at them with a scornful smile, seeming to say, "You will not frighten this fellow."

A month later, the sailor Bloom died in a way that Mrs. Wallis found almost as distressing as he apparently did:

> Bernardo died about eleven o'clock, P.M. He continued irritable and impatient till the last. A few hours before his death some warm tea was offered him, and, finding that he could not swallow it, he spit it from his mouth, and threw the cup from him in the most spiteful manner. He was continually angry with God that he did not end his sufferings, and take him to heaven. What an awful state in which to leave the world! as though a man might curse and swear, practise every impurity, and then go to heaven at death. What would heaven be with such spirits, who die blaspheming their Maker! (Wallis 1983 [1851]: 263–269)

9. John 20:11–17 states:

> But Mary stood without at the sepulchre weeping: and as she wept, she stooped down, and looked into the sepulchre, And seeth two angels in white sitting, the one at the head, and the other at the feet, where the body of Jesus had lain. And they say unto her, Woman, why weepest thou? She saith unto them, Because they have taken away my Lord, and I know not where they have laid him. And

when she had thus said, she turned herself back, and saw Jesus standing, and knew not that it was Jesus. Jesus saith unto her, Woman, why weepest thou? whom seekest thou? She, supposing him to be the gardener, saith unto him, Sir, if thou have borne him hence, tell me where thou hast laid him, and I will take him away. Jesus saith unto her, Mary. She turned herself, and saith unto him, Rabboni; which is to say, Master. Jesus saith unto her, Touch me not; for I am not yet ascended to my Father: but go to my brethren, and say unto them, I ascend unto my Father, and your Father; and to my God, and your God.

Reuben's narrative echoes this one in several ways. When observers, including Bulu, thought that Reuben was dead, "he opened his eyes, and lifting up his hand he beckoned us to be silent, saying 'Weep not, weep not'" (Bulu 1871: 52). Frightened, one man explained, "we are weeping because of your death," and Reuben admonished him, "Weep not for me...weep for yourselves. As for me, I live" (52). Consciously or not, the dying Reuben—or at least Bulu's version of Reuben (and the translator's version of Bulu)—was imitating Jesus's resurrection.

10. Stewards (*tuirara*) are Methodist officials who represent the church to the *vanua* (chiefs and people) and vice versa. The word he used was *vesu*, meaning "to bind, tie a person...to arrest" (Capell 1991: 262). In context, it seemed to mean that the late chief was trying to grab him.

11. A reviewer for an earlier version of this chapter observed how the dream's "naming" of the late chief's enemies—by showing them dragging him away—echoes the old tradition of a person pronouncing enemies' names from a deathbed. In addition, Allen Abramson (2005: 337) notes that in Fijian understandings, "Many or, quite possibly, all chiefs are killed by sorcerers."

12. Barbara Herr notes that indigenous "Fijians believe in soul departure during dreams and hence believe that what they think and feel and do in dreams are 'real' experiences of the soul (*yalo*), encountering as it does in its nocturnal wanderings both the souls of other living persons (*yalo bula*), good and evil, and numerous other spirit entities (*tevoro*)" (1981: 333–334; see also Herr 1983). Thus, while the dreamer's intentions might not matter, it is difficult in Fijian understandings to dismiss his vision as "just a dream."

13. Minor corrections and improvements have been made to the texts originally published in *American Ethnologist* 34(4).

14. Pamela Ballinger (personal communication, June 8, 2006) suggests that a communal ethic raises a possible alternative interpretation of my friend's playing the tape at a kava session. He was not worried about the content of the story itself but about the implications of being seen to work alone. In this regard, consider the work of David Akin, who has argued that political discourse among the Kwaio (Solomon Islands) focuses attention on the declining observance of taboos. For Kwaio, taboos are considered to have been violated only when knowledge of the violation is made public. Because ancestors are considered to be the

ever-present invisible audience for public discussions, "People complain that the ideas harped on in public meetings have hampered their ability…to keep [taboos and violations as] private, personal affairs" (Akin n.d.: 7). In other words, discourse about managing a supposedly "proper balance" between public and private has recalibrated the fractal distinctions between publicity and privacy for the Kwaio, making the latter an anxious and seemingly ever-diminishing domain. See also Akin 2003.

CHAPTER 5

1. Bakhtin (1981: 337); Philippa McDonald, "Interview with Fiji's Interim Prime Minister, Commodore Frank Bainimarama," abc.net.au, August 3, 2010.

2. On the earliest statement, see Ratuva (2007: 35); on the latest, see "Fiji Army Boss Says 'No Coup,'" fijilive.com, November 2, 2006.

3. McDonald, "Interview."

4. See Sera Janine, "What Coup: FHRC," *Fiji Times*, August 31, 2007, p.1. Shameem took various actions in support of Bainimarama which, to some observers, seemed to mock the idea of human rights (see Green 2013: 199–200, 205–206). For example, when opponents of the government were intimidated, sometimes with physical violence, she dismissed their claims by arguing that "many of the protestors were 'not genuine pro-democracy activists,'" as if this excused their abuse (Fraenkel 2007: 434). On Father Barr's defense of the coup, see Paulo Baleinakorodawa, Kevin Barr, and Semiti Qalowasa, "Time of Uncertainty, Opportunity," fijitimes.com, December 19, 2006.

5. "New Media Decree Effective Immediately," fijilive.com, June 28, 2010.

6. "Bainimarama Has Destroyed Talks: Qarase," fijilive.com, April 9, 2009.

7. See sections 6.3.64 and 7.2.90 of Fiji's 1997 constitution (ICL 2000); see also Newbury (2006) for a historical overview of the council.

8. Michael McKenna, "Fiji Army Chief in Renewed Threat," theaustralian.com.au, November 22, 2006.

9. On the number of officials charged, see "Cases Consolidated for 27 Ministers," fijilive.com, March 23, 2010. On the standing committee meeting, see "Police Charge Church Ministers," *Fiji Sun*, February 5, 2010, p. 3. In January 2012, the government issued the Public Order (Amendment) Decree 2012, a set of amendments to the original Public Order ordinance of 1969. The 2012 version inserted elements from the emergency regulations such as those giving police the power to cancel or forbid public meetings and controlling the movements of people deemed a threat to public order (compare Fiji Government 1969, 2009, 2012). Whereas the 1969 Public Order Act stated that religious meetings did not need official permits, the 2012 act repealed this exemption.

10. Sean Dorney, "Just the Good News, Thanks," newmatilda.com, May 19, 2009. Beginning on December 30, 2006, the *Times* ran a banner across the top of

its front page each day with italicized white letters on a red background reading " 'We Will Uphold Media Freedom'—Cmdr Bainimarama's Promise." This
referred to a statement Bainimarama had made the day after his coup. The banner remained in place for almost 500 days, but was dropped when publisher
Evan Hannah was deported on May 2, 2008.

11. "Man Gets on Bus," *Fiji Daily Post*, April 15, 2009, p. 2; "Curfew Rumours
Untrue: Leweni," and "Man Goes Out," *Fiji Daily Post*, April 17, 2009, p. 2;
I have edited the punctuation in quoting these articles.

12. " 'Death Threats Will Not Deter Me,' " *Fiji Times*, August 2, 2007, p. 1.

13. Reijeli Kikau, "Qarase Death Threat Claim," *Fiji Times*, August 29, 2007, p. 1.

14. Philip Dorling, "Fiji's Iron Fist," *The Age* (Melbourne), August 27, 2011,
pp. 18–19.

15. McDonald, "Interview"; ellipses in original.

16. This understanding of language resonates to some extent with that of US
Marines drill instructors as described by Catherine Hicks Kennard (2006).
She observes that male and female drill instructors cultivate different ways of
speaking that are meant to instill a "sense of urgency" in soldiers: men speak
quickly and loudly in order "to obtain a fast and accurate recruit response"
and women speak directly and confidently, although not necessarily more
quickly or loudly, to achieve the same results (Hicks Kennard 2006: 136). The
one-way nature of this kind of communication is reinforced by the rule that
drill instructors can refer to themselves in the first person whereas recruits
must refer to themselves and their instructors in the third person which,
Hicks Kennard argues, is meant to elevate group membership above individual identity while marking and reinforcing drill instructors' authority over
recruits (2006: 61–62).

17. Vasiti Ritova, "Why Narube's Gone: Leweni," *Fiji Sun*, April 16, 2009, p. 3.

18. Dorney, "Just the Good News, Thanks." Moreover, in June 2009 the government began publishing its own biweekly newspaper, *New Dawn*, a resolutely
upbeat production with cheerfully misleading stories. *New Dawn* is an apt illustration of Andrew Arno's point that "pro-social news media" with a positive
slant is "evidently yearned for by so many in power" (2009: 173). Arno offers an
example in which "Russian journalists employed by the Russian News Service,
a major private company that provides newscasts for the Russian Radio network, began to struggle with a new rule according to which '50 percent of the
news must be positive, regardless of what cataclysm might befall Russia on any
given day' " (Arno 2009: 9; the embedded quotation comes from a *New York
Times* article by Andrew E. Kramer).

19. Paul McGeough, "Fear and Loathing in Fiji," *The Age* (Melbourne), November
28, 2009, p. 3 of "Insight" section.

20. The document's official title does not include an apostrophe in "Peoples,"
although journalists sometimes insert one.

21. Petero Mataca, "We Got [*sic*] to Keep on Moving," *Fiji Times*, January 23, 2007, p. 7. The council originally had forty-five members, with "National Task Teams" and "Working Groups" targeting particular topics (NCBBF 2008b: i–ii). The NCBBF's "Technical Director" was John Samy, a former consultant for the Asian Development Bank who "played the key behind-the-scenes role" in developing the Charter (Fraenkel 2008: 456).

22. Of the changes that were made, some seem to have been proposed by interest groups. For example, the final version recommends: "Enhance, support and ensure the participation of women leaders at all levels of decision making" (NCBBF 2008b: 21); this does not appear in the draft version. Some changes are rhetorical, as when the draft's negative statement "Our Public Sector... is inefficient and ineffective" becomes the positive "Our Public Sector... must be efficient and effective" (NCBBF 2008a: 20; 2008b: 23). The most significant change comes in a recommendation on the parallel system of governance. In Fiji, multiethnic and democratic government stands alongside a special division for indigenous affairs. The draft recommends that these systems be integrated at the level of provinces, of which Fiji has fourteen; the final version recommends integration at the higher level of divisions, of which Fiji has four.

23. Mazzarella (2006: 476), analyzing Indian politics, describes the discourse of "e-governance" as an effort "to synthesize a political language of transparency with a corporate managerial vision."

24. After the opening, the authors—writing as "We, the People of Fiji"—declare their support for the existing constitution, calling it "the supreme law of our country" which they "seek to strengthen" (2008b: 2). The next section is called "Foundation for the Common Good Based on Our Shared Values, Vision and Principles." It begins with a declaration of faith in a universal God, and affirms "the freedom of our various communities to follow their beliefs as enshrined in our Constitution" (2008b: 3). The final introductory section, "Moving Forward Together," contains sunny-day platitudes ("We, the people of Fiji, must come together, join hands, and work together") along with a statement placing the military at the center of future governments: "We strongly endorse that [*sic*] a holistic approach to human security be adopted by our Security Forces as the basis of the democratic state and the institutions for national security" (2008b: 5, 7). The charter's concluding sections then include two pages on implementation and two pages titled "Commitments and Pledge." One commitment is "To support the Constitution and this the Peoples Charter as the foundation for rebuilding our Nation as one country, as one people"; another reaffirms the central role of the military in Fiji's future democracy (2008b: 41). The concluding pledge is a collision between a prayer and a high school yearbook: "we place our faith in God and our people's humanity to help us fulfil these commitments in the time of our lives" (2008b: 42).

25. The eleven pillars are as follows:
    1. Ensuring Sustainable Democracy and Good and Just Governance
    2. Developing a Common National Identity and Building Social Cohesion
    3. Ensuring Effective, Enlightened and Accountable Leadership
    4. Enhancing Public Sector Efficiency, Performance Effectiveness and Service Delivery
    5. Achieving Higher Economic Growth While Ensuring Sustainability
    6. Making More Land Available for Productive and Social Purposes
    7. Developing an Integrated Development Structure at the Divisional Level
    8. Reducing Poverty to a Negligible Level by 2015
    9. Making Fiji a Knowledge-based Society
    10. Improving Health Service Delivery
    11. Enhancing Global Integration and International Relations

26. Serafina Silaitoga and Amelia Vunileba, "Rabuka Rues," *Fiji Times*, May 15, 2008, p. 1.

27. Iliesa Tora, "One-Vote System 'Way to Go,'" fijidailypost.com, September 30, 2007 (this site is no longer online).

28. "Fiji to Top Pacific Forum Agenda," fijilive.com, October 9, 2007; Sabra Lane, "Fiji Expels Envoys over Interference Claims," abc.net.au, November 4, 2009.

29. In the Fijian translation of the Peoples Charter, the phrase "coup culture" is rendered differently in each instance. In the first, it is given as *na matetaka ni vuaviri*, meaning "the epidemic of coups"; in the second, it receives a more direct translation, *i tovo ni noda Vanua na vuaviri*, "our people's culture [or custom of our land] is coups" (NCBBF 2008d: 9). In the third, it becomes *na veitarataravi ni vuaviri*, "the succession of coups" (2008d: 30).

30. This quotation was published in "End 2000 Coup Probe," a *Fiji Daily Post* article posted on December 10, 2003, at fijilive.com; it is no longer available online.

31. Wadan Narsey, "The Charter Charade," *Fiji Times*, December 23, 2008, p. 7. In April 2008, the *Fiji Times* ran a text-message survey asking whether the charter would be good for Fiji. Obviously, such a survey draws on a narrow segment of Fiji's population and is open to multiple voting, and is therefore not an especially reliable result. Nonetheless, the numbers were intriguingly close: 46.2 percent (761 responses) said no and 45.8 percent (755) said yes, with 130 responses unclear; see "Majority Say No to Charter, but 'Ayes' Close Behind," *Fiji Times*, April 15, 2008, p. 3.

32. Serafina Qalo, "Charter Rejected," *Fiji Times*, August 30, 2007, p. 4; see also "Methodists Reject Role in Charter," *Fiji Times*, January 29, 2008, p. 4. The letter of June 2007 contains two points of special interest. First, the authors note that although the government claimed to be soliciting the public's response to their plans, "the decision to proceed with them [has] already been taken unilaterally by the interim government," suggesting that "the call for public submission is…merely a pretense to garner public support for what in reality

are unilaterally imposed policy measures" (Methodist Church in Fiji and the Association of Christian Churches in Fiji 2007: 3–4). In other words, appeals to dialogue were a strategy for facilitating monologue. Second, the authors express their concern—presciently, it turns out—that the charter would help the government get rid of the constitution: "We learn from recent experience in Thailand that the military junta had abrogated the constitution and had similarly appointed a body [working] towards a people's charter that will be the basis of such [*sic*] country's next constitution. We are concerned that through the proposed charter, the interim regime will undermine constitutional rule and the rule of law here in Fiji" (2007: 4–5).

33. Mary Rauto, "Methodists Oppose Charter," *Fiji Times*, August 27, 2008, p. 2.

34. Narsey, "The Charter Charade"; see also Newland 2009.

35. See, e.g., "Catholic Group Petitions Rome," *Fiji Times*, October 30, 2007, p. 3; "Catholics Support Methodists," *Fiji Times*, August 28, 2008, p. 2.

36. Amelia Vunileba, "People Will Have Final Say on What Is in Charter," fijitimes. com, February 16, 2008.

37. "Wardens Guided by Charter Pillars," *Fiji Times*, June 6, 2009, p. 5.

38. For the Nandan quotation, see Frederica Elbourne, "Academic Refers to Charter as Scared [*sic*]," fijitimes.com, June 21, 2008. For the Bainimarama quotation, see Maria Burese, "Frankly Speaking with Voreqe," fijitimes.com, October 21, 2007.

39. Robert Matau, "Voreqe: Church Sows Racial Hate," *Fiji Times*, October 31, 2007, p. 1.

40. For other uses of Romans 13:1–2 in Fijian public discourse, see Heinz (1993: 420); Kaplan (1990: 141); Tomlinson (2013); and Tui Rakuita, "The Veneer of a General Will," *Fiji Times*, June 12, 2008, p. 7.

41. My casual visits to government offices in Suva to see if they were distributing copies of the charter showed that some offices were not doing so. This could mean that they had given away all of their copies, of course, but the perplexed responses I received from workers at several offices when I asked for a copy led me to believe that charter distribution might never have been a widespread activity.

CHAPTER 6

1. On the 1985 ceremonies, see "Thousands March to Mark Church's 150th Anniversary," *Fiji Times*, August 19, 1985, p. 2; Gasolo Vuetivavalagi, "A Candle-lit Final Rally," *Fiji Times*, August 26, 1985, p. 1. In addition, several years earlier an American Anglican priest had "suggested to the villagers that a Mass of Reconciliation be held on the mound that marks the spot where [Baker] was killed" (Fischer 1981: 25). The villagers thought this was a good idea. In June 1977 the Catholic Archbishop Petero Mataca led a party of pilgrims on a ten-day

walk through Vitilevu's interior, apparently in imitation of Baker's journey, and then conducted the Mass at the site (Fischer 1981: 24-26).

2. See, e.g., Bush (2000), Toko (2007), Tomlinson (2012b), and Timoci Vula, "Kaba Seeks Church Forgiveness," *Daily Post*, August 28, 2003, p. 5.

3. In the Fijian original, "O cei e liu? Na lotu se na vanua? O cei e dodonu me liu tiko? Na lotu se na vanua? E dua na ka me'u vakadeitaka: guilecava na vosa na 'lotu'; guilecava na vosa na 'vanua'. Rawa ni da kaya e muri na lotu; e muri na vanua; e liu duadua ga na Kalou." For a discussion of this passage, see Tomlinson (2009: 97–98).

4. Nayacakalou and Ravuvu wrote about the *vanua* at different historical moments, with the former writing before the heyday of ethnonationalist politics and the latter fully wrapped up in them. But they had personal motivations, too, for taking their different stances. Nayacakalou was a commoner by birth who was generally not supported by chiefs in his pursuit of education overseas (he completed his dissertation at the University of London, under Raymond Firth's supervision, in 1964). He was also attuned to the mid-twentieth-century discourse of development and modernization, linking it with Firth's scholarly interests in structural change; Nayacakalou even accompanied the geographer Oskar Spate on a trip to Fiji that resulted in a report urging Fijians to become more individualistic. For these reasons, Nayacakalou's perspective on chiefs' future role in Fijian society was decidedly critical, and his corresponding view of the *vanua* was not a romantic or reverential one, but an academic and pragmatic one (Tomlinson 2006b). Ravuvu criticized chiefs, too, but as indicated in the earlier quotation, he also glorified the *vanua* in quasi-mystical terms. He endorsed ethnonationalist discourse, writing that individualism, democracy, and egalitarianism were "foreign imposition[s]" that had weakened indigenous Fijians' "position and rights in their country of heritage" (Ravuvu 1991: 98). Although Nayacakalou and Ravuvu were born within several years of each other and both worked as academic anthropologists, their careers came to very different ends. In 1969, Nayacakalou was chosen to manage the Native Land Trust Board, an institution in the politically delicate position of overseeing and potentially reforming land ownership regulations. The stress of the job was immense, and he died of his third heart attack at age forty-four in 1972. Ravuvu, who had taught at the University of the South Pacific for many years, became a senator in the last years of his life, and died at age seventy-seven in 2008 ("Academic Dies, 77," fijitimes.com, March 13, 2008).

5. In the wake of Fiji's coups, many non-Fijian anthropologists have felt it necessary to analyze transformations in understandings of the *vanua*; see, e.g., Brison (2007); Kaplan (1990, 1995); Rutz (1995); Ryle (2010); Tomlinson (2009); Toren (1995); and Williksen-Bakker (1990). One work that deserves special mention is Annelise Riles's analysis of the divergent views of land held by a "Part-European clan," the Whippys, who have lived in Fiji since their

ancestor David arrived from Nantucket in the 1820s (Riles 2000: 92–113). The Suva-based Whippys believe that the land held by their rural kin in Vanualevu, who subdivide their landholdings each generation, had "gone small." Those in Vanualevu, however, "repeatedly asserted that 'nothing changes' or 'nothing has happened'" (95). Riles uses the contrast to explore broader themes of information, sociality, and network forms, explaining that for the rural Whippys, "division is an exercise in verification, a rehearsal of the given truth, as much as a principle of kinship or ownership.... [A]lthough the passing of time was marked by division, nothing was added or taken away, in the endless repetition of this process, from the prefigured whole" (107–108). In terms of *vanua* discourse, the urban Whippys emphasize the threat of loss through diminution whereas the rural Whippys emphasize the land's timeless character. Although seemingly opposed, these two strands are firmly intertwined in national discourse.

6. Such spiritual warfare is a common practice in the movement known as "Third wave evangelism" (Jorgensen 2005). Methodists have cannily adopted these practices for their own purposes. As Newland explains for a village in Naitasiri, "Methodists are appropriating the concept of cleansing or purification that is central to Pentecostal teaching in an attempt to incorporate the Pentecostals back into the village under Methodist authority" (2004: 14–15).

7. In the Fijian text, "E sega ni i naki ni i vola oqo me sosomitaka na I Vola Tabu Vou ka da vakayagataka tiko e daidai. E gadrevi ga me rawa ni da wilika talega na i vola ka ogataka vakalevu o Oniti, ka me da raica na totoka ni nona vakadewa," and "... ka vakadewa vakadodonu saraga mai na vosa Vakirisi ki na vosa Vakaviti."

8. The interview was conducted in English. In this quotation, I have made minor edits for clarity.

9. For the translation and a description of the project, see nftbible.com.

Bibliography

[No listed author]. 1999. Tukutuku Lekaleka me Baleti Baidamudamu (Short Information about Baidamudamu). In Ai Tuvatuva ni Soqo ni Kena Curumi ka Vakatabui ni Valenilotu "Kenisareti" (Program for the Opening and Consecration of Kenisareti [Gennesaret] Church), April 3, 1999. Document in author's possession.

Abbott, Andrew. 2001. *Chaos of Disciplines*. Chicago: University of Chicago Press.

Abramson, Allen. 2005. Drinking to Mana and Ethnicity: Trajectories of Yaqona Practice and Symbolism in Eastern Fiji. *Oceania* 75(4): 325–341.

Agha, Asif. 2007. *Language and Social Relations*. Cambridge: Cambridge University Press.

Ahern, Emily M. 1979. The Problem of Efficacy: Strong and Weak Illocutionary Acts. *Man* 14(1): 1–17.

Akin, David. 2003. Concealment, Confession, and Innovation in Kwaio Women's Taboos. *American Ethnologist* 30(3): 381–400.

Akin, David. N.d. Ancestral Publics and Private Transgressions in a Solomon Islands Society. Paper presented at the 104th Annual Meeting of the American Anthropological Association, Washington, DC, December 3, 2005.

Allen, William. 1892. Kadavu Circuit Report. Methodist Missionary Society of Australia Collection, National Archives of Fiji.

Anderson, Allan. 2004. *An Introduction to Pentecostalism: Global Charismatic Christianity*. Cambridge: Cambridge University Press.

Aporosa, S. 2013. *Yaqona (Kava) and Education in Fiji: Investigating "Cultural Complexities" from a Post-Development Perspective*. Ph.D. dissertation, Massey University, Palmerston North, New Zealand.

Appadurai, Arjun. 1996. *Modernity at Large: Cultural Dimensions of Globalization*. Minneapolis: University of Minnesota Press.

Appadurai, Arjun. 2006. *Fear of Small Numbers: An Essay on the Geography of Anger*. Durham, NC: Duke University Press.

Ariès, Philippe. 1981. *The Hour of Our Death*, trans. H. Weaver. London: Penguin.

Arno, Andrew. 1985. Impressive Speeches and Persuasive Talk: Traditional Patterns of Political Communication in Fiji's Lau Group from the Perspective of Pacific Ideal Types. *Oceania* 56(2): 124–137.

Arno, Andrew. 1990. Disentangling Indirectly: The Joking Debate in Fijian Social Control. In *Disentangling: Conflict Discourse in Pacific Societies*, ed. K. A. Watson-Gegeo and G. M. White, pp. 241–289. Stanford, CA: Stanford University Press.

Arno, Andrew. 1993. *The World of Talk on a Fijian Island: An Ethnography of Law and Communicative Causation*. Norwood, NJ: Ablex.

Arno, Andrew. 2003. Aesthetics, Intuition, and Reference in Fijian Ritual Communication: Modularity in and out of Language. *American Anthropologist* 105(4): 807–819.

Arno, Andrew. 2009. *Alarming Reports: Communicating Conflict in the Daily News*. New York: Berghahn Books.

Atkinson, Jane Monnig. 1989. *The Art and Politics of Wana Shamanship*. Berkeley: University of California Press.

Austin, J. L. 1975. *How to Do Things with Words*, 2nd ed., ed. J. O Urmson and M. Sbisà. Cambridge, MA: Harvard University Press.

Bakhtin, Mikhail. 1981. Discourse in the Novel. In *The Dialogic Imagination: Four Essays by M. M. Bakhtin*, ed. M. Holquist, trans. C. Emerson and M. Holquist, pp. 259–422. Austin: University of Texas Press.

Bakhtin, Mikhail. 1984. *Problems of Dostoevsky's Poetics*, ed. and trans. C. Emerson. Minneapolis: University of Minnesota Press.

Bakhtin, Mikhail. 1986. *Speech Genres and Other Late Essays*, ed. C. Emerson and M. Holquist, trans. V.W. McGee. Austin: University of Texas Press.

Baleiwaqa, Tevita. 1987. Setareki Akeai Tuilovoni and the Young People's Department of the Methodist Church in Fiji (1951–1967). Project Report for the Bachelor of Divinity degree, Pacific Theological College, Suva.

Barber, Karin. 2007. *The Anthropology of Texts, Persons and Publics*. New York: Cambridge University Press.

Barber, Paul. 1988. *Vampires, Burial, and Death: Folklore and Reality*. New Haven, CT: Yale University Press.

Bateson, Gregory. 1935. Culture Contact and Schismogenesis. *Man* 35 (December): 178–183.

Bauman, Richard. 1986. *Story, Performance, and Event: Contextual Studies of Oral Narrative*. Cambridge: Cambridge University Press.

Bauman, Richard, and Charles Briggs. 1990. Poetics and Performance as Critical Perspectives on Language and Social Life. *Annual Review of Anthropology* 19: 59–88.

Becker, Anne E. 1995. *Body, Self, and Society: The View from Fiji*. Philadelphia: University of Pennsylvania Press.

Bell, Catherine. 1992. *Ritual Theory, Ritual Practice*. New York: Oxford University Press.

Belshaw, Cyril S. 1964. *Under the Ivi Tree: Society and Economic Growth in Rural Fiji*. Berkeley: University of California Press.

Besnier, Niko. 2009. *Gossip and the Everyday Production of Politics*. Honolulu: University of Hawai'i Press.

Bialecki, Jon. 2011. No Caller ID for the Soul: Demonization, Charisms, and the Unstable Subject of Protestant Language Ideology. *Anthropological Quarterly* 84(3): 679–704.

Birtwhistle, Allen. 1954. *In His Armour: The Life of John Hunt of Fiji*. London: Cargate Press.

Brenneis, Donald. 1990. Dramatic Gestures: The Fiji Indian *Pancayat* as Therapeutic Event. In *Disentangling: Conflict Discourse in Pacific Societies*, ed. K. A. Watson-Gegeo and G. M. White, pp. 214–238. Stanford, CA: Stanford University Press.

Briggs, Charles L. 1988. *Competence in Performance: The Creativity of Tradition in Mexicano Verbal Art*. Philadelphia: University of Pennsylvania Press.

Brison, Karen J. 2007. *Our Wealth Is Loving Each Other: Self and Society in Fiji*. Lanham, MD: Lexington Books.

Brown, Jr., Calvin S. 1891. Other Dialectal Forms in Tennessee. *PMLA* 6(3): 171–175.

Brown, Peter. 1981. *The Cult of the Saints: Its Rise and Function in Latin Christianity*. Chicago: University of Chicago Press.

Bulu, Joeli. 1871. *Joel [sic] Bulu: The Autobiography of a Native Minister in the South Seas*. "A Missionary," trans. G. S. Rowe. London: Wesleyan Mission House.

Bush, Joseph E. 2000. Land and Communal Faith: Methodist Belief and Ritual in Fifi [sic]. *Studies in World Christianity* 6(1): 21–37.

Capell, A. 1991. *A New Fijian Dictionary*, 3rd ed. Suva: Government Printer.

Cargill, David. 1977. *The Diaries and Correspondence of David Cargill, 1832–1843*, ed. A. J. Schütz. Canberra: Australian National University Press.

Chang, Jung. 2004. *Wild Swans: Three Daughters of China*. London: Harper Perennial.

Cheng, Nien. 1986. *Life and Death in Shanghai*. London: Grafton Books.

Clammer, John R. 1973. Colonialism and the Perception of Tradition in Fiji. In *Anthropology and the Colonial Encounter*, ed. T. Asad, pp. 199–220. New York: Humanities Press.

Clark, Jeffrey. 2000. *Steel to Stone: A Chronicle of Colonialism in the Southern Highlands of Papua New Guinea*. Oxford: Oxford University Press.

Clifford, James. 1997. *Routes: Travel and Translation in the Late Twentieth Century*. Cambridge, MA: Harvard University Press.

Coleman, Simon. 2000. *The Globalisation of Charismatic Christianity: Spreading the Gospel of Prosperity*. Cambridge: Cambridge University Press.

Coleman, Simon. 2006. When Silence Isn't Golden: Charismatic Speech and the Limits of Literalism. In *The Limits of Meaning: Case Studies in the Anthropology of Christianity*, ed. M. Engelke and M. Tomlinson, pp. 39–61. New York: Berghahn.

Collocott, Alfred J. 1882. Kadavu Circuit Annual Report. Methodist Missionary Society of Australia Collection, National Archives of Fiji.

Comaroff, Jean, and John Comaroff. 1993. Introduction. In *Modernity and Its Malcontents: Ritual and Power in Postcolonial Africa*, ed. J. and J. Comaroff, pp. xi–xxxvii. Chicago: University of Chicago Press.

Comaroff, Jean, and John Comaroff. 1999. Occult Economies and the Violence of Abstraction: Notes from the South African Postcolony. *American Ethnologist* 26(2): 279–303.

Curulala, Malakai C. 1974. *The Liturgical Movement and the Renewal of Worship in the Methodist Church in Fiji*. Project Report for the Bachelor of Divinity degree, Pacific Theological College, Suva.

Daidoji Yuzan. 1988. *The Code of the Samurai*, trans. A. L. Sadler. Rutland, VT: Charles E. Tuttle.

Dean, Eddie, and Stan Ritova. 1988. *Rabuka: No Other Way*. Sydney: Doubleday.

Deane, W. 1921. *Fijian Society: Or the Sociology and Psychology of the Fijians*. London: Macmillan.

Degei, Sekove Bigitibau. 2007. *The Challenge to Fijian Methodism—The Vanua, Identity, Ethnicity and Change*. Master of Social Sciences thesis, University of Waikato, Hamilton, New Zealand.

de Witte, Marleen. 2011. Touched by the Spirit: Converting the Senses in a Ghanaian Charismatic Church. *Ethnos* 76(4): 489–509.

Diaz, Vicente M., and J. Kehaulani Kauanui. 2001. Native Pacific Cultural Studies on the Edge. *Contemporary Pacific* 13(2): 315–341.

Dix, Gregory. 1945. *The Shape of the Liturgy*. Westminster, UK: Dacre Press.

Duranti, Alessandro, and Charles Goodwin, eds. 1992. *Rethinking Context: Language as an Interactive Phenomenon*. Cambridge: Cambridge University Press.

Eisenlohr, Patrick. 2010. Materialities of Entextualization: The Domestication of Sound Reproduction in Mauritian Muslim Devotional Practices. *Journal of Linguistic Anthropology* 20(2): 314–333.

Evans-Pritchard, E. E. 1956. *Nuer Religion*. Oxford: Clarendon Press.

Fa'asi'i, Urima. 1993. Gospel and Culture in the *Ava* Ceremony. *Pacific Journal of Theology* 10: 61–63.

Faleali'i, Tele'a Logoleo V. 1998. *God in the Ava Ceremony: A Theological Reflection from One Polynesian Context*. Master of Theology thesis, Pacific Theological College, Suva.

Feld, Steven. 1982. *Sound and Sentiment: Birds, Weeping, Poetics, and Song in Kaluli Expression*. Philadelphia: University of Pennsylvania Press.

Field, Michael, Tupeni Baba, and Unaisi Nabobo-Baba. 2005. *Speight of Violence: Inside Fiji's 2000 Coup*. Canberra: Pandanus Books.

Fiji Bureau of Statistics. 2007. Reports on the 2007 census, archived at www.statsfiji. gov.fj/index.php/2007-census-of-population, accessed October 22, 2013.

Fiji Government. 1969. Laws of Fiji, Chapter 20: Public Order, archived at www.fiji. gov.fj, accessed February 5, 2012.

Fiji Government. 2009. Public Emergency Regulations 2009. *Republic of Fiji Islands Government Gazette* 10(5): 11–18.

Fiji Government. 2012. Public Order (Amendment) Decree 2012, archived at www. fiji.gov.fj, accessed February 5, 2012.

Fiji One National News [television program]. 2008. Broadcast of November 16. Digital copy in author's possession.

Fischer, Edward. 1981. *Fiji Revisited: A Columban Father's Memories of Twenty-Eight Years in the Islands.* New York: Crossroad.

Fox, James J. 2011. Old Christians among Christian Moderns. Paper presented at the Australian Anthropological Society meetings, Perth, July 5–8.

Fraenkel, Jon. 2007. The Fiji Coup of December 2006: Who, What, Where and Why? In *From Election to Coup in Fiji: The 2006 Campaign and Its Aftermath,* ed. J. Fraenkel and S. Firth, pp. 420–449. Canberra: ANU E Press.

Fraenkel, Jon. 2008. Fiji. *The Contemporary Pacific* 20(2): 450–460.

Fraenkel, Jon. 2009. The Great Roadmap Charade. Electoral Issues in Post-Coup Fiji. In *The 2006 Military Takeover in Fiji: A Coup to End All Coups?,* ed. J. Fraenkel, S. Firth, and B.V. Lal, pp. 155–184. Canberra: ANU E Press.

Fraenkel, Jon. 2010. Fiji. *The Contemporary Pacific* 22(2): 416–433.

France, Peter. 1966. The Kaunitoni Migration: Notes on the Genesis of a Fijian Tradition. *Journal of Pacific History* 1: 107–113.

France, Peter. 1969. *The Charter of the Land: Custom and Colonization in Fiji.* Melbourne: Oxford University Press.

Gal, Susan. 2002. A Semiotics of the Public/Private Distinction. *differences* 13(1): 77–95.

Gal, Susan. 2005. Language Ideologies Compared: Metaphors of Public/Private. *Journal of Linguistic Anthropology* 15(1): 23–27.

Gal, Susan, and Kathryn Woolard, eds. 2001. *Languages and Publics: The Making of Authority.* Manchester, UK: St. Jerome.

Gao, Yuan. 1987. *Born Red: A Chronicle of the Cultural Revolution.* Stanford, CA: Stanford University Press.

Gardner, D. S. 1983. Performativity in Ritual: The Mianmin Case. *Man* 18(2): 346–360.

Geraghty, Paul. 1977. How a Myth Is Born—The Story of the Kaunitoni Story. *Mana* 2(1): 25–29.

Geraghty, Paul. 1993. Pulotu, Polynesian Homeland. *Journal of the Polynesian Society* 102(4): 343–384.

Geschiere, Peter. 1997. *The Modernity of Witchcraft: Politics and the Occult in Postcolonial Africa.* Charlottesville: University of Virginia Press.

Goffman, Erving. 1981. *Forms of Talk.* Philadelphia: University of Pennsylvania Press.

Goodman, Felicitas D. 1972. *Speaking in Tongues: A Cross-Cultural Study of Glossolalia.* Chicago: University of Chicago Press.

Gordillo, Gastón R. 2004. *Landscapes of Devils: Tensions of Place and Memory in the Argentinean Chaco*. Durham, NC: Duke University Press.

Green, Michael. 2013. *Persona Non Grata: Breaking the Bond, Fiji and New Zealand 2004–2007*. Auckland: Dunmore.

Green, Roger C. 1991. Near and Remote Oceania—Disestablishing "Melanesia" in Culture History. In *Man and a Half: Essays in Pacific Anthropology and Ethnobiology in Honour of Ralph Bulmer*, ed. A Pawley, pp. 491–502. Auckland: Polynesian Society.

Greenblatt, Stephen. 2010. Cultural Mobility: An Introduction. In *Cultural Mobility: A Manifesto*, pp. 1–23. Cambridge: Cambridge University Press.

Grimshaw, Beatrice. 1907. *Fiji and Its Possibilities*. New York: Doubleday, Page.

Gunson, Niel. 1994. British Missionaries and Their Contribution to Science in the Pacific Islands. In *Darwin's Laboratory: Evolutionary Theory and Natural History in the Pacific*, ed. R. MacLeod and P. F. Rehbock, pp. 283–316. Honolulu: University of Hawai`i Press.

Hale, Horatio. 1968 [1846]. *United States Exploring Expedition: Ethnography and Philology*. Ridgewood, NJ: Gregg Press.

Hanks, W. F. 1989. Text and Textuality. *Annual Review of Anthropology* 18: 95–127.

Hau'ofa, Epeli. 1980. Blood in the Kava Bowl. In *Lali: A Pacific Anthology*, ed. A. Wendt, pp. 239–240. Auckland: Longman Paul.

Hau'ofa, Epeli. 1994. Our Sea of Islands. *The Contemporary Pacific* 6(1): 148–161.

Hau'ofa, Epeli. 2008. *We Are the Ocean: Selected Works*. Honolulu: University of Hawai'i Press.

Heatley, E. M. 1923. The Invisible Isle of Burotu. *Transactions of the Fijian Society for the Year 1922*, pp. 10–11.

Heinz, Donald. 1993. The Sabbath in Fiji as Guerrilla Theatre. *Journal of the American Academy of Religion* 61(3): 415–442.

Herr, Barbara. 1981. The Expressive Character of Fijian Dream and Nightmare Experiences. *Ethos* 9(4): 331–352.

Herr, Barbara. 1983. *Gender and Illness among Lauan Fijians: Somatic and Affective Disorder*. Ph.D. dissertation, University of California–Los Angeles.

Hicks Kennard, Catherine. 2006. *Gender and Command: A Sociophonetic Analysis of Female and Male Drill Instructors in the United States Marine Corps*. Ph.D. dissertation, University of Arizona.

Hocart, A. M. 1912. A Native Fijian on the Decline of His Race. *Hibbert Journal* 11(1): 85–98.

Hocart, A. M. 1929. *Lau Islands, Fiji*. Honolulu: Bernice P. Bishop Museum.

ICL [International Constitutional Law]. 2000. Fiji Constitution. http://www.servat.unibe.ch/icl/fj00000_.html, accessed December 23, 2011.

IG-Fiji. 2009. The Snake in Priests [sic] Clothing. igfiji.blogspot.com/2009/01/snake-in-priests-clothing.html, January 24; accessed February 9, 2009.

Jacobsen, Douglas. 2003. *Thinking in the Spirit: Theologies of the Early Pentecostal Movement*. Bloomington: Indianapolis University Press.

Jakobson, Roman. 1990 [1965]. Quest for the Essence of Language. In *On Language*, ed. L. R. Waugh and M. Monville-Burston, pp. 407–421. Cambridge, MA: Harvard University Press.

Jorgensen, Dan. 2005. Third Wave Evangelism and the Politics of the Global in Papua New Guinea: Spiritual Warfare and the Recreation of Place in Telefolmin. *Oceania* 75(4): 444–461.

Kaplan, Martha. 1990. Christianity, People of the Land, and Chiefs in Fiji. In *Christianity in Oceania: Ethnographic Perspectives*, ed. J. Barker, pp. 127–147. Lanham, MD: University Press of America.

Kaplan, Martha. 1995. *Neither Cargo nor Cult: Ritual Politics and the Colonial Imagination in Fiji*. Durham, NC: Duke University Press.

Kaplan, Martha, and John D. Kelly. 1994. Rethinking Resistance: Dialogics of Disaffection in Colonial Fiji. *American Ethnologist* 21(1): 123–151.

Kaplan, Martha, and John D. Kelly. 1999. On Discourse and Power: "Cults" and "Orientals" in Fiji. *American Ethnologist* 26(4): 843–863.

Keane, Webb. 1995. The Spoken House: Text, Act, and Object in Eastern Indonesia. *American Ethnologist* 22(1): 102–124.

Keane, Webb. 1997. *Signs of Recognition: Powers and Hazards of Representation in an Indonesian Society*. Berkeley: University of California Press.

Keane, Webb. 2002. Sincerity, "Modernity," and the Protestants. *Cultural Anthropology* 17(1): 65–92.

Keane, Webb. 2003. Semiotics and the Social Analysis of Material Things. *Language and Communication* 23(3–4): 409–425.

Keane, Webb. 2006. Anxious Transcendence. In *The Anthropology of Christianity*, ed. F. Cannell, pp. 308–323. Durham, NC: Duke University Press.

Keane, Webb. 2007. *Christian Moderns: Freedom and Fetish in the Mission Encounter*. Berkeley: University of California Press.

Keane, Webb. 2010. Minds, Surfaces, and Reasons in the Anthropology of Ethics. In *Ordinary Ethics: Anthropology, Language, and Action*, ed. M. Lambek, pp. 64–83. New York: Fordham University Press.

Kelly, John D. 1991. *A Politics of Virtue: Hinduism, Sexuality, and Countercolonial Discourse in Fiji*. Chicago: University of Chicago Press.

Kelly, John D., and Martha Kaplan. 1990. History, Structure, and Ritual. *Annual Review of Anthropology* 19: 119–150.

Kennedy, George A. 1991, ed. and trans. *Aristotle, On Rhetoric: A Theory of Civic Discourse*. New York: Oxford University Press.

Kertzer, David I. 1988. *Ritual, Politics, and Power*. New Haven, CT: Yale University Press.

Kirch Patrick Vinton. 1997. *The Lapita Peoples: Ancestors of the Oceanic World*. Malden, MA: Blackwell.

Kotobalavu, Jioji. 2009. Resolving the Current Crisis in Fiji—A Personal Perspective. In *The 2006 Military Takeover in Fiji: A Coup to End All Coups?*, ed. J. Fraenkel, S. Firth, and B. V. Lal, pp. 375–384. Canberra: ANU E Press.

Kuipers, Joel C. 1992. Obligations to the Word: Ritual Speech, Performance, and Responsibility among the Weyewa. In *Responsibility and Evidence in Oral Discourse*, ed. J. H. Hill and J. T. Irvine, pp. 88–104. Cambridge: Cambridge University Press.

Kulick, Don. 2003. No. *Language and Communication* 23(2): 139–151.

Kuru, Etuate M. 1994. *God's Word in Water: A Re-Statement of Christian Baptism in the Fijian Context*. Master of Theology thesis, Pacific Theological College, Suva.

Lal, Brij V. 1992. *Broken Waves: A History of the Fiji Islands in the Twentieth Century*. Honolulu: University of Hawaii Press.

Lal, Brij V. 2000a. Rabuka of Fiji: Coups, Constitutions and Confusion. *Journal of Pacific History* 35(3): 319–326.

Lal, Brij V. 2000b. A Time to Change: The Fiji General Elections of 1999. In *Fiji before the Storm: Elections and the Politics of Development*, ed. B. V. Lal, pp. 21–47. Canberra: Asia Pacific Press.

Lal, Brij V. 2004. Heartbreak Islands: Reflections on Fiji in Transition. In *Law and Empire in the Pacific: Fiji and Hawai'i*, ed. S. E. Merry and D. Brenneis, pp. 261–280. Santa Fe, NM: School of American Research Press.

Lal, Brij V. 2009. "This Process of Political Readjustment": The Aftermath of the 2006 Fiji Coup. In *The 2006 Military Takeover in Fiji: A Coup to End All Coups?*, ed. J. Fraenkel, S. Firth, and B. V. Lal, pp. 67–93. Canberra: ANU E Press.

Lal, Brij V. 2011. *Intersections: History, Memory, Discipline*. Lautoka, Fiji, and Sydney: Fiji Institute of Applied Studies and Asia Pacific Publications.

Langham, Frederick. n.d.. Notebook, c. 1877–1895, MOM Collection, Mitchell Library, Sydney, CY reel 3578.

Laugrand, Frédéric, and Jarich Oosten. 2007. Reconnecting People and Healing the Land: Inuit Pentecostal and Evangelical Movements in the Canadian Eastern Arctic. *Numen* 54(3): 229–269.

Lester, R. H. 1941. Kava Drinking in Vitilevu, Fiji, Part I. *Oceania* 12(2): 97–121.

Lewis, E. D. n.d. Death by Mischants and Cooking for the Dead: Chiasmus and Inversion in Tana Ai Ritual. In *Chiasmus in the Drama of Life*, ed. B. Wiseman and A. Paul. Forthcoming.

Lienhardt, Godfrey. 1961. *Divinity and Experience: The Religion of the Dinka*. Oxford: Clarendon Press.

Luhrmann, T.M. 2012. *When God Talks Back: Understanding the American Evangelical Relationship with God*. New York: Alfred A. Knopf.

Mannheim, Bruce, and Dennis Tedlock. 1995. Introduction. In *The Dialogic Emergence of Culture*, ed. D. Tedlock and B. Mannheim, pp. 1–32. Urbana: University of Illinois Press.

Manoa, Pio. 2010. Redeeming Hinterland. *Pacific Journal of Theology* 43: 65–86.

Mara, Ratu Sir Kamisese. 1997. *The Pacific Way: A Memoir*. Honolulu: University of Hawai'i Press.

Mara, Tevita Uluilakeba. 2011. Regime Change Should Happen in Fiji Soon. coup-fourandahalf.com/2011/05/roko-ului-in-tonga-media-statement.html, May 14; accessed October 21, 2013.

Marsh, Ngaio. 1997. *Artists in Crime*. New York: St. Martin's Paperbacks.

Mazzarella, William. 2006. Internet X-Ray: E-Governance, Transparency, and the Politics of Immediation in India. *Public Culture* 18(3): 473–505.

McGrath, Thomas B. 1973. Sakau in Towm, Sarawi in Towm. *Oceania* 44(1): 64–67.

McKenzie, Andrea. 2003. Martyrs in Low Life? Dying "Game" in Augustan England. *Journal of British Studies* 42: 167–205.

Meo, Iliesa Jovili. 1973. *The Role of the Laity in the Church and Its Implications for the Life of the Methodist Church in Fiji*. B.D. thesis, Pacific Theological College, Suva.

Methodist Church in Fiji and the Association of Christian Churches in Fiji. 2007. Submission on Interim Government's "Peoples Charter for Change & Progress," June 12. Document in author's possession.

Methodist Overseas Mission Trust Association. 1938. *Ai Vola ni Sere ni Lotu Wesele e Viti* (Fijian Hymn Book).

Miyazaki, Hirokazu. 2004. *The Method of Hope: Anthropology, Philosophy, and Fijian Knowledge*. Stanford, CA: Stanford University Press.

Moore, Sally Falk. 1977. Political Meetings and the Simulation of Unanimity: Kilimanjaro 1973. In *Secular Ritual*, ed. S. F. Moore and B. G. Myerhoff, pp. 151–172. Assen, Netherlands: Van Gorcum.

Murray, A.W. 1888. *The Bible in the Pacific*. London: James Nisbet.

Nabobo-Baba, Unaisi. 2006a. *Knowing and Learning: An Indigenous Fijian Approach*. Suva: Institute of Pacific Studies, University of the South Pacific.

Nabobo-Baba, Unaisi. 2006b. A Place to Sit (and Stand), Vugalei Fijian Epistemology: An Exploration into Teaching and Learning and Ways of Knowing of a Particular Cultural Group. In *Dreadlocks Vaka Vuku*, ed. M. Prasad, pp. 48–59. Suva: Pacific Writing Forum, University of the South Pacific.

Narsey, Wadan, Toga Raikoti, and Epeli Waqavonovono. 2010. Preliminary Report: Poverty and Household Incomes in Fiji in 2008–09. Suva: Fiji Islands Bureau of Statistics, http://www.spc.int/prism/fjtest/cens&surveys/Preliminary%20Report%20on%20the%202008-09%20HIES%20.pdf; accessed October 22, 2013.

Nayacakalou, R. R. 1961. Traditional Authority and Religious Sanctions in Fiji. Unpublished seminar paper delivered at the London School of Economics, November 3. Manuscript in author's possession.

Nayacakalou, R. R. 1975. *Leadership in Fiji*. Melbourne: Oxford University Press.

Nayacakalou, R. R. 1978. *Tradition and Change in the Fijian Village*. Suva: South Pacific Social Sciences Association and Institute of Pacific Studies, University of the South Pacific.

NCBBF (National Council for Building a Better Fiji). 2008a. *Peoples Charter for Change, Peace and Progress (Draft)*. Suva: Government Printing Department.

NCBBF (National Council for Building a Better Fiji). 2008b. *Peoples Charter for Change, Peace and Progress.* Suva: Government Printing Department.

NCBBF (National Council for Building a Better Fiji). 2008c. *The State of the Nation and the Economy Report: Executive Summary.* Suva: Government Printing Department.

NCBBF (National Council for Building a Better Fiji). 2008d. Na Yavutu ni Veisau kei na Toso ki Liu ni Lewe i Viti [Fijian translation of Peoples Charter for Change, Peace and Progress]. Suva: Government Printing Department.

Nettleton, Joseph. 1906. *John Hunt: Pioneer Missionary and Saint.* London: C. H. Kelly.

Newbury, Colin. 2006. *Bose Vakaturaga:* Fiji's Great Council of Chiefs, 1875–2000. *Pacific Studies* 29(1–2): 82–127.

Newland, Lynda. 2004. Turning the Spirits into Witchcraft: Pentecostalism in Fijian Villages. *Oceania* 75(1): 1–18.

Newland, Lynda. 2007. The Role of the Assembly of Christian Churches in Fiji in the 2006 Elections. In *From Election to Coup in Fiji: The 2006 Campaign and Its Aftermath,* ed. J. Fraenkel and S. Firth, pp. 300–314. Canberra: ANU E Press.

Newland, Lynda. 2009. Religion and Politics: The Christian Churches and the 2006 Coup in Fiji. In *The 2006 Military Takeover in Fiji: A Coup to End All Coups?,* eds. J. Fraenkel, S. Firth, and B.V. Lal, pp. 187–207. Canberra: ANU E Press.

Nolan, Howard. 1896. Kadavu Circuit Report. Methodist Missionary Society of Australia Collection, National Archives of Fiji.

Nunn, Patrick D. 2009. *Vanished Islands and Hidden Continents of the Pacific.* Honolulu: University of Hawai'i Press.

Ohnuki-Tierney, Emiko. 2002. *Kamikaze, Cherry Blossoms, and Nationalisms: The Militarization of Aesthetics in Japanese History.* Chicago: University of Chicago Press.

Ortner, Sherry B. 2006. *Anthropology and Social Theory: Culture, Power, and the Acting Subject.* Durham, NC: Duke University Press.

Orwell, George. 2000 [1946]. How the Poor Die. In *Essays,* pp. 387–396. London: Penguin.

Osorio, Jonathan Kay Kamakawiwo`ole. 2002. *Dismembering Lahui: A History of the Hawaiian Nation to 1887.* Honolulu: University of Hawai`i Press.

Parmentier, Richard J. 1987. *The Sacred Remains: Myth, History, and Polity in Belau.* Chicago: University of Chicago Press.

Peters, John Durham. 1999. *Speaking into the Air: A History of the Idea of Communication.* Chicago: University of Chicago Press.

Pigliasco, Guido Carlo. 2010. We Branded Ourselves Long Ago: Intangible Cultural Property and Commodification of Fijian Firewalking. *Oceania* 80(2): 161–181.

Pigliasco, Guido Carlo. 2012. "Are They Evil?": Denominational Competition and Cultural Demonization on a Fijian Island. *People and Culture in Oceania* 28: 45–68.

Polglase, Mary. 1858. Letter to Miss Camplin, from Lakemba, Fiji, September 9. In *Occasional Paper no. 1 of the Ladies' Committee for Ameliorating the Condition of Women in Heathen Countries, Female Education, &c*, pp. 25–27. MOM Collection, Mitchell Library, Sydney, reel FM4/1799.

Premdas, Ralph R. 1995. *Ethnic Conflict and Development: The Case of Fiji*. Aldershot, UK: Avebury.

Quain, Buell. 1948. *Fijian Village*. Chicago: University of Chicago Press.

Rafael, Vicente L. 1988. *Contracting Colonialism: Translation and Christian Conversion in Tagalog Society under Early Spanish Rule*. Ithaca, NY: Cornell University Press.

Rafael, Vicente L. 2009. *Conjuración*/Conspiracy in the Philippine Revolution of 1896. In *Words in Motion: Toward a Global Lexicon*, ed. C. Gluck and A. L. Tsing, pp. 219–239. Durham, NC: Duke University Press.

Rappaport, Roy A. 1999. *Ritual and Religion in the Making of Humanity*. Cambridge: Cambridge University Press.

Ratuva, Steven. 2002. God's Will in Paradise: The Politics of Ethnicity and Religion in Fiji. *Development Bulletin* 59: 19–23.

Ratuva, Steven. 2007. The Pre-Election "Cold War": The Role of the Fiji Military during the 2006 Election. In *From Election to Coup in Fiji*, ed. J. Fraenkel and S. Firth, pp. 26–45. Canberra: ANU E Press.

Ratuvili, Sitiveni. 1971. *The Career and Thought of Irenaeus of Lyons, with Special Reference to the Bearing of His Teaching about Church, Scripture and Tradition on the Present Situation of Fiji Methodism*. B.D. thesis, Pacific Theological College, Suva.

Ravuvu, Asesela D. 1983. *Vaka i Taukei: The Fijian Way of Life*. Suva: Institute of Pacific Studies, University of the South Pacific.

Ravuvu, Asesela D. 1991. *The Facade of Democracy: Fijian Struggles for Political Control, 1830–1987*. Suva: Reader Publishing House.

Reed, William. 1888. *Recent Wanderings in Fiji: Glimpses of Its Villages, Churches, and Schools*. London: T. Woolmer.

Riles, Annelise. 2000. *The Network Inside Out*. Ann Arbor: University of Michigan Press.

Robbins, Joel. 2001a. God Is Nothing but Talk: Modernity, Language, and Prayer in a Papua New Guinea Society. *American Anthropologist* 103(4): 901–912.

Robbins, Joel. 2001b. Ritual Communication and Linguistic Ideology: A Reading and Partial Reformulation of Rappaport's Theory of Ritual. *Current Anthropology* 42(5): 591–599.

Robbins, Joel. 2004. *Becoming Sinners: Christianity and Moral Torment in a Papua New Guinea Society*. Berkeley: University of California Press.

Robbins, Joel. 2009. Is the *Trans-* in Transnational the *Trans-* in Transcendent? On Alterity and the Sacred in the Age of Globalization. In *Transnational Transcendence: Essays on Religion and Globalization*, ed. T. J. Csordas, pp. 55–71. Berkeley: University of California Press.

Rockefeller, Stuart Alexander. 2011. "Flow." *Current Anthropology* 52(4): 557–578.

Rokowaqa, Epeli. 1926. Ai Tukutuku kei Viti. *Methodist Missionary Magazine* (April), pp. 1–84.

Rosner, Brian S. 1995. "That Pattern of Teaching": Issues and Essays in Pauline Ethics. In *Understanding Paul's Ethics: Twentieth-Century Approaches*, ed. B. S. Rosner, pp. 1–23. Grand Rapids, MI: Eerdmans.

Rumsey, Alan. 2004. Ethnographic Macro-Tropes and Anthropological Theory. *Anthropological Theory* 4(3): 267–298.

Rutz, Henry J. 1995. Occupying the Headwaters of Tradition: Rhetorical Strategies of Nation Making in Fiji. In *Nation Making: Emergent Identities in Postcolonial Melanesia*, ed. R. J. Foster, pp. 71–93. Ann Arbor: University of Michigan Press.

Ryle, Jacqueline. 2001. *My God, My Land: Interwoven Paths of Christianity and Tradition in Fiji.* Ph.D. dissertation, School of Oriental and African Studies, University of London.

Ryle, Jacqueline. 2010. *My God, My Land: Interwoven Paths of Christianity and Tradition in Fiji.* Farnham, Surrey: Ashgate.

Sahlins, Marshall. 1962. *Moala: Culture and Nature on a Fijian Island.* Ann Arbor: University of Michigan Press.

Sahlins, Marshall. 1985. *Islands of History.* Chicago: University of Chicago Press.

Sahlins, Marshall. 1991. The Return of the Event, Again; With Reflections on the Beginnings of the Great Fijian War of 1843 to 1855 between the Kingdoms of Bau and Rewa. In *Clio in Oceania: Toward a Historical Anthropology*, ed. A. Biersack, pp. 37–99. Washington, DC: Smithsonian Institution Press.

Sahlins, Marshall. 1996. The Sadness of Sweetness: The Native Anthropology of Western Cosmology. *Current Anthropology* 37(3): 395–428.

Sahlins, Marshall. 2004. *Apologies to Thucydides: Understanding History as Culture and Vice Versa.* Chicago: University of Chicago Press.

Samarin, William J. 1972. *Tongues of Men and Angels: The Religious Language of Pentecostalism.* New York: Macmillan.

Sapir, Edward. 1924. Culture, Genuine and Spurious. *American Journal of Sociology* 29(4): 401–429.

Sax, William S. 2010. Ritual and the Problem of Efficacy. In *The Problem of Ritual Efficacy*, ed. W. S. Sax, J. Quack, and J. Weinhold, pp. 3–16. New York: Oxford University Press.

Schieffelin, Edward L. 1985. Performance and the Cultural Construction of Reality. *American Ethnologist* 12(4): 707–724.

Schieffelin, Edward L. 1996. On Failure and Performance: Throwing the Medium Out of the Seance. In *The Performance of Healing*, ed. C. Laderman and M. Roseman, pp. 59–89. New York: Routledge.

Schieffelin, Edward L. 1998. Problematizing Performance. In *Ritual, Performance, Media*, ed. F. Hughes-Freedland, pp. 194–207. Abingdon, UK: Routledge.

Seemann, Berthold. 1973. *Viti: An Account of a Government Mission to the Vitian or Fijian Islands, 1860–1861.* Folkestone and London: Dawsons of Pall Mall.

Seruvakula, Semi B. 2000. *Bula Vakavanua*. Suva: Institute of Pacific Studies, University of the South Pacific.

Sherzer, Joel. 1987. A Discourse-Centered Approach to Language and Culture. *American Anthropologist* 89(2): 295–309.

Shoaps, Robin. 1999. The Many Voices of Rush Limbaugh: The Use of Transposition in Constructing a Rhetoric of Common Sense. *Text* 19(3): 399–437.

Shoaps, Robin. 2002. "Pray Earnestly": The Textual Construction of Personal Involvement in Pentecostal Prayer and Song. *Journal of Linguistic Anthropology* 12(1): 34–71.

Silverstein, Michael. 1981. The Limits of Awareness. Austin: Southwest Educational Development Laboratory, Sociolinguistic Working Paper #84.

Silverstein, Michael. 1992. The Uses and Utility of Ideology: Some Reflections. *Pragmatics* 2(3): 311–323.

Silverstein, Michael. 2003. *Talking Politics: The Substance of Style from Abe to "W."* Chicago: Prickly Paradigm Press.

Silverstein, Michael. 2004. "Cultural" Concepts and the Language-Culture Nexus. *Current Anthropology* 45(5): 621–652.

Silverstein, Michael, and Greg Urban. 1996. The Natural History of Discourse. In *Natural Histories of Discourse*, ed. M. Silverstein and G. Urban, pp. 1–17. Chicago: University of Chicago Press.

Srebrnik, Henry. 2002. Ethnicity, Religion, and the Issue of Aboriginality in a Small Island State: Why Does Fiji Flounder? *The Round Table* 364: 187–210.

Stasch, Rupert. 2011. Ritual and Oratory Revisited: The Semiotics of Effective Action. *Annual Review of Anthropology* 40: 159–174.

Stasch, Rupert. 2012. Afterword: On Relationality of Codes and the Indexical Iconicity of Linguistic Otherness within Wider Value Formations. *Australian Journal of Anthropology* 23(3): 398–405.

Sudnow, David. 1967. *Passing On: The Social Organization of Dying*. Englewood Cliffs, NJ: Prentice-Hall.

Tabana ni Vosa kei Na iTovo Vakaviti [Institute of Fijian Language and Culture]. 2005. *Na i Volavosa Vakaviti* [Fijian Dictionary]. Suva: Institute of Fijian Language and Culture.

Tambiah, Stanley Jeyaraja. 1985 [1979]. A Performative Approach to Ritual. In S. J. Tambiah, *Culture, Thought, and Social Action: An Anthropological Perspective*. Cambridge, MA: Harvard University Press.

Taofinu'u, Pio. 1995. *O Le 'Ava O Se Pelofetaga: The Kava Ceremony Is a Prophecy*, rev. ed. Apia: Archdiocese of Western Samoa.

Teaiwa, Katerina Martina. 2005. Our Sea of Phosphate: The Diaspora of Ocean Island. In *Indigenous Diasporas and Dislocations*, ed. G. Harvey and C. D. Thompson Jr., pp. 169–191. Aldershot, UK: Ashgate.

Teaiwa, Teresia K. 1998. Yaqona/Yagoqu: Roots and Routes of a Displaced Native. *UTS Review* 4(1): 92–106.

Teaiwa, Teresia K. 2005. The Classroom as a Metaphorical Canoe: Co-operative Learning in Pacific Studies. *World Indigenous Nations Higher Education Consortium Journal* 2005: 38–48.

Tengan, Ty P. Kāwika, Tēvita O. Ka'ili, and Rochelle Tuitagava'a Fonoti. 2010. Genealogies: Articulating Indigenous Anthropology in/of Oceania. *Pacific Studies* 33(2–3): 139–167.

Thomas, Nicholas. 1986. *Planets around the Sun: Dynamics and Contradictions of the Fijian Matanitu*. Sydney: University of Sydney.

Thomas, Nicholas. 1997. *In Oceania: Visions, Artifacts, Histories*. Durham: Duke University Press.

Thompson, Laura. 1940. *Southern Lau, Fiji: An Ethnography*. Honolulu: Bernice P. Bishop Museum.

Thomson, Basil. 1895. The Kalou-Vu (Ancestor-Gods) of the Fijians. *Journal of the Anthropological Institute of Great Britain and Ireland* 24: 340–359.

Thomson, Basil. 1968 [1908]. *The Fijians: A Study of the Decay of Custom*. London: Dawsons of Pall Mall.

Thornley, Andrew. 2000. *The Inheritance of Hope: John Hunt, Apostle of Fiji*. Suva: Institute of Pacific Studies, University of the South Pacific.

Thornley, Andrew. 2002. *Exodus of the I Taukei: The Wesleyan Church in Fiji: 1848–74*. Suva: Institute of Pacific Studies, University of the South Pacific.

Thornley, Andrew. 2005. *A Shaking of the Land: William Cross and the Origins of Christianity in Fiji*. Suva: Institute of Pacific Studies, University of the South Pacific.

Thornley, Andrew, Ilaitia Sevati Tuwere, and Tauga Vulaono, eds. 2007. *Na Kosipeli i Maciu kei Marika: Me Vaka e Volai e Na i Matai ni I Vola Tabu Vou (1847) ka Vakadewataka o Na i Talatala Joni Oniti. [The Gospel of Matthew and Mark: As Written in the First New Testament (1847) Translated by Rev. John Hunt.]* Suva: Methodist Church in Fiji and Rotuma.

Tippett, A. R. 1954. *The Christian (Fiji 1835–67)*. Auckland: Institute Printing and Publishing Society.

Tippett, A. R. 1976. The Metaanthropology of Conversion in Non-Western Society. In The Phenomenology of Cross-Cultural Conversion in Oceania, pp. 83–147. Unpublished manuscript in the Tippett Collection, St. Mark's National Theological Centre Library, Canberra. [Originally printed as Research in Progress Pamphlet no. 14, Fuller Theological Seminary, Pasadena, 1976.]

Toko, Apete. 2007. *The Role of the Methodist Church in Fiji and Rotuma in Discovering Pathways to Reconciliation in Fiji's Context of Coups*. Master of Theology thesis, Pacific Theological College, Suva.

Tomlinson, Matt. 2002. *Voice and Earth: Making Religious Meaning and Power in Christian Fiji*. Ph.D. dissertation, University of Pennsylvania.

Tomlinson, Matt. 2004. Ritual, Risk, and Danger: Chain Prayers in Fiji. *American Anthropologist* 106(1): 6–16.

Tomlinson, Matt. 2006a. The Limits of Meaning in Fijian Methodist Sermons. In *The Limits of Meaning: Case Studies in the Anthropology of Christianity*, ed. M. Engelke and M. Tomlinson, pp. 129–146. New York: Berghahn.

Tomlinson, Matt. 2006b. Reflexivity, Tradition, and Power: The Work of R. R. Nayacakalou. *Ethnos* 71(4): 489–506.

Tomlinson, Matt. 2009. *In God's Image: The Metaculture of Fijian Christianity*. Berkeley: University of California Press.

Tomlinson, Matt. 2012a. God Speaking to God: Translation and Unintelligibility at a Fijian Pentecostal Crusade. *Australian Journal of Anthropology* 23(3): 274–289.

Tomlinson, Matt. 2012b. Passports to Eternity: Whales' Teeth and Transcendence in Fijian Methodism. In *Flows of Faith: Religious Reach and Community in Asia and the Pacific*, ed. L. Manderson, W. Smith, and M. Tomlinson, pp. 215–231. Dordrecht: Springer.

Tomlinson, Matt. 2013. The Generation of the Now: Denominational Politics in Fijian Christianity. In *Christian Politics in Oceania*, ed. M. Tomlinson and D. McDougall, pp. 78–102. New York: Berghahn.

Toren, Christina. 1988. Making the Present, Revealing the Past: The Mutability and Continuity of Tradition as Process. *Man* (n.s.) 23(4): 696–717.

Toren, Christina. 1990. *Making Sense of Hierarchy: Cognition as Social Process in Fiji*. London: Athlone Press.

Toren, Christina. 1995. Seeing the Ancestral Sites: Transformations in Fijian Notions of the Land. In *The Anthropology of Landscape*, ed. E. Hirsch and M. O'Hanlon, pp. 163–183. Oxford: Clarendon Press.

Toren, Christina. 1998. Cannibalism and Compassion: Transformations in Fijian Concepts of the Person. In *Common Worlds and Single Lives: Constituting Knowledge in Pacific Societies*, ed. V. Keck, pp. 95–115. Oxford: Berg.

Toren, Christina. 1999. *Mind, Materiality, and History: Explorations in Fijian Ethnography*. London: Routledge.

Toren, Christina. 2004. Becoming a Christian in Fiji: An Ethnographic Study of Ontogeny. *Journal of the Royal Anthropological Institute* 10(1): 222–240.

Toren, Christina. 2009. Intersubjectivity as Epistemology. *Social Analysis* 53(2): 130–146.

Trnka, Susanna. 2008. *State of Suffering: Political Violence and Community Survival in Fiji*. Ithaca: Cornell University Press.

Tsing, Anna Lowenhaupt. 2005. *Friction: An Ethnography of Global Connection*. Princeton, NJ: Princeton University Press.

Tuwere, Ilaitia S. 1992. *Making Sense of Vanua (Land) in the Fijian Context: A Theological Exploration*. Ph.D. thesis, Melbourne College of Divinity.

Tuwere, Ilaitia S. 2001. Indigenous Peoples' Struggle for Land and Identity. *Pacific Journal of Theology* 25: 39–50.

Tuwere, Ilaitia S. 2002. *Vanua: Towards a Fijian Theology of Place*. Suva and Auckland: Institute of Pacific Studies at the University of the South Pacific and College of St. John the Evangelist.

Urban, Greg. 1996. Entextualization, Replication, and Power. In *Natural Histories of Discourse*, ed. M. Silverstein and G. Urban, pp. 21–44. Chicago: University of Chicago Press.

Urban, Greg. 2001. *Metaculture: How Culture Moves through the World*. Minneapolis: University of Minnesota Press.

Urban, Greg. 2010. A Method for Measuring the Motion of Culture. *American Anthropologist* 112(1): 122–139.

Urban, Greg, and Kristin M. Smith. 1998. The Sunny Tropics of "Dialogue"? *Semiotica* 121(3–4): 263–281.

Vakadewavosa, Epineri. 1991. *Comparative Analysis of the Viwa Model of the Teaching Ministry and the Methodist Church in Fiji Today*. Project Report for the Bachelor of Divinity degree, Pacific Theological College, Suva.

Wacker, Grant. 1984. The Functions of Faith in Primitive Pentecostalism. *Harvard Theological Review* 77(3–4): 353–375.

Wallis, Mary. ["A Lady."] 1983 [1851]. *Life in Feejee: Or, Five Years among the Cannibals*. Suva: Fiji Museum.

Warner, Michael. 2002. *Publics and Counterpublics*. New York: Zone.

Warren, Samuel. 1827. *Chronicles of Wesleyan Methodism*, vol. 1. London: John Stephens.

Waterhouse, Joseph. 1997 [1866]. *The King and People of Fiji*. Auckland: Pasifika Press.

Waterhouse, Joseph. n.d. *History of Fiji*. Unpublished MS, Alexander Turnbull Library, Wellington.

Webb, A. J. 1870. Letter from Kadavu, Fiji, December 1869. *Wesleyan Missionary Notices* 3 [sic] 2(13): 202–205.

Weir, Christine. 1998. Fiji and the Fijians: Two Modes of Missionary Discourse. *Journal of Religious History* 22(2): 152–167.

Welch, John W. 1981a. Chiasmus in the New Testament. In *Chiasmus in Antiquity: Structures, Analyses, Exegeses*, ed. J. W. Welch, pp. 211–249. Provo, UT: Research Press at Brigham Young University.

Welch, John W. 1981b. Introduction. In *Chiasmus in Antiquity: Structures, Analyses, Exegeses*, ed. J. W. Welch, pp. 9–16. Provo, UT: Research Press at Brigham Young University.

Wendt, Albert. 1976. Towards a New Oceania. *Mana Review* 1(1): 49–60.

Wesley, Charles. 1756. *The Cause and Cure of Earthquakes: A Sermon Preach'd from Psalm xlvi.8. Occasioned by the Earthquake on March 8, 1750*, 2nd ed. London: n.p. Accessed through "Eighteenth Century Collections Online," galenet.galegroup. com, October 30, 2007.

White, Geoffrey M. 1991. *Identity through History: Living Stories in a Solomon Islands Society*. Cambridge: Cambridge University Press.

White, Geoffrey M. 2013. Chiefs, Church, and State in Santa Isabel, Solomon Islands. In *Christian Politics in Oceania*, ed. M. Tomlinson and D. McDougall, pp. 171–197. New York: Berghahn.

White, Joseph. 1867a. Letter from Kadavu, Fiji, September 15, 1866. *Wesleyan Missionary Notices* 1(38): 609.

White, Joseph. 1867b. Letter from Kadavu, Fiji, June 5, 1866. *Wesleyan Missionary Notices* 1(38): 609–610.

Whorf, Benjamin. 1956. *Language, Thought, and Reality: Selected Writings of Benjamin Lee Whorf.* Cambridge, MA: MIT Press.

Whyte, Martin King. 1974. *Small Groups and Political Rituals in China.* Berkeley: University of California Press.

Williams, George. 2008. *Qarase v Bainimarama* and the Rule of Law in Fiji. In "Courts and Coups in Fiji: The 2008 High Court Judgment in Qarase v Bainimarama," ed. G. Williams, G. Leung, A. J. Regan, and J. Fraenkel, pp. 2–6. Canberra: RSPAS/SSGM Discussion Paper #10 of 2008.

Williams, Thomas. 1982 [1858]. *Fiji and the Fijians,* vol. 1, ed. G. S. Rowe. Suva: Fiji Museum.

Williksen-Bakker, Solrun. 1990. Vanua—A Symbol with Many Ramifications in Fijian Culture. *Ethnos* 55 (3–4): 232–247.

Wilson, Cecil. 1905. Article on the Melanesian Mission's Work in Melanesia. *Southern Cross Log,* 11 April.

Wirtz, Kristina. 2005. "Where Obscurity Is a Virtue": The Mystique of Unintelligibility in Santería Ritual. *Language and Communication* 25(4): 351–375.

Wirtz, Kristina. 2007. Making Sense of Unintelligible Messages in Divine Communication. *Text and Talk* 27(4): 435–462.

Wolffe, John. 2000. *Great Deaths: Grieving, Religion, and Nationhood in Victorian and Edwardian Britain.* Oxford: Oxford University Press.

Wolterstorff, Nicholas. 1995. *Divine Discourse: Metaphysical Reflections on the Claim That God Speaks.* Cambridge: Cambridge University Press.

Wood, A. Harold. 1978. *Overseas Missions of the Australian Methodist Church, Volume II: Fiji.* Melbourne: Aldersgate Press.

Wright, Cliff, ed. 1979. *Seeds of the Word: Tongan Culture and Christian Faith.* No listed publisher; typescript in University of Auckland library.

Young, Michael W. 1995. Kava and Christianity in Central Vanuatu. *Canberra Anthropology* 18(1–2): 61–96.

Zuo, Jiping. 1991. Political Religion: The Case of the Cultural Revolution in China. *Sociological Analysis* 52(1): 99–110.

Index